Australian Heritage Needlework

Victoriana

Ribbonwork, Whitework, Beadwork, Lace and Crochet

Contributors

**Mary Dufour, Jean Hinder, Heather Joynes, Marie Laurie,
Patricia R. McDonald, June Powys, Margot Riley, Lindie Ward**

Series Editor Jennifer Sanders

A Lothian Book

Acknowledgements

All illustrations credited to the Museum of Applied Arts and Sciences, Sydney, appear by courtesy of the trustees of the museum.

The authors and publishers would like to acknowledge the assistance of the institutions who so kindly gave access to their collections and for permission for us to reproduce patterns in the five volumes of *Australian Heritage Needlework*. All sources of objects are acknowledged alongside the photographs. Thanks are also due to those who gave access to objects in private collections.

Angela Lober and Antonia Creese prepared the graphs for all counted thread work; Jan Düttmer prepared all other illustrations.

Special thanks to Heather Joynes and Pat Langford for advice and Marie Cavanagh at the Embroiderers Guild NSW Inc., and Toni Lober for permission to reproduce the table of threads for counted thread work.

Thanks also to Jane Hylton at the Art Gallery of South Australia; Johnsie Adam, Beulah Brusetti, Betty Riley, Mrs C McQuade, Mr McOlive, Moreen and Josephine Clark, Stephanie Schrapel, Sonia Perry, Annette Butterfield, Mr Stuchbery; Peter Emmett at Elizabeth Bay House and the Historic Houses Trust; Ann Toy at the Police and Justice Museum; Myra Stanbury at the Western Australian Maritime Museum; Catherine Snowdon and Jane de Teliga at the Art Gallery of NSW; Glynis Jones, Christina Sumner and Ja Patterson at the Museum of Applied Arts and Sciences; Alison Melrose, Peter Mercer and Helen McWhirter at the Tasmanian Museum and Art Gallery; Wanda McPherson at the Embroiderers Guild of Victoria; Marie Gebhart and Narelle Grieve of the Quilters Guild; Julie Henning of the Cavalcade of Fashion; Maureen Holbrook at the Embroiderers Guild of South Australia; Robert Cousens at Coats-Semco; Sue Frost at Campbell Conservation; Mr Little at Blundell's Farm House; John Gowty at Buda; and Glenda King at the Queen Victoria Museum and Art Gallery.

A LOTHIAN BOOK

LOTHIAN PUBLISHING COMPANY PTY LTD
A division of Thomas C. Lothian Pty Ltd
11 Munro Street, Port Melbourne, Victoria 3207

First published 1993
© Copyright Sandpiper Press 1993

National Library of Australia
Cataloguing-in-publication data:

Victoriana: ribbonwork, whitework, beadwork, lace and crochet.
ISBN 0 85091 593 7.

1. Needlework —.Patterns. 2. Decoration and ornament — Victorian style. 3. Embroidery — Patterns. 4. Crocheting — Patterns. 5. Ribbon work. I. Sanders, Jennifer. (Series: Australian heritage needlework series).

A SANDPIPER PRESS PRODUCTION
Published in association with Sandpiper Press (NSW) Pty Ltd
2 Trebor Street, Pennant Hills, NSW 2120

Managing Editor Meryl Potter
Illustrated by Jan Düttmer
Designed by Di Quick
Printed in Hong Kong through Colorcraft Ltd
Cover: Chrysanthemum panel and ribbons in the collection of the Embroiderers Guild NSW Inc.,
Photograph by David Liddle

Contents

Introduction

Jennifer Sander

In the early years of settlement, making and repairing clothing and furnishings was an essential and time-consuming task at the end of what was, for most women, a hard-working day. The limited availability of ready-made goods, isolation from retail outlets, a harsh environment and rough way of life, the need to save money for essentials that had to be bought, and the shortage of needlewomen all conspired to make needlework the constant companion of women from all classes of society. This need for the material things of daily life meant that proficiency in needlework was an essential skill for the women of the European settlement of Australia.

The ladies, daughters and house servants, as well as the governess, were expected to contribute to a household's needlework tasks. However, references to 'fancy articles' and 'fancywork' in various sources indicate that not all needlework was plain sewing. The technological revolution that later saw the invention and commercial production of the sewing machine also saw the rise in popularity of women's domestic handicrafts, collectively known as 'fancywork'. The journals of nineteenth century women also often record that they made needlework gifts for each other and their friends. Not only was this an acceptable occupation when not mending or making useful things such as curtains, but distance from shops and women's limited personal income would also have made needlework the best solution to the need for personal gifts.

Fancywork was initially the province of wealthier women like the Wentworths, Macarthurs and Macleays. However, it soon became the chief leisuretime occupation of thousands of Australian women in the later nineteenth and early twentieth centuries.

Increased wealth in the colony, particularly from the discovery of gold and the export of wool, saw the rise of the middle class. With money to purchase manufactured goods and labour-saving devices, such as the sewing machine, as well as to hire servants, the women of the house had time for decorative rather than utilitarian needlework. Growth in trade and local manufacturing industries meant that household linen and furnishings and ready-made clothing could be more readily purchased. Even those who lived in the bush could order goods using mail-order catalogues published by the larger shopping emporiums such as Anthony Horderns and Farmers.

The term 'fancywork' encompasses all manner of work from traditional embroidery to novelties such as wax flowers, ribbonwork, shellwork, beetle-wing embroidery, seaweed pictures, leatherwork and feather pictures. Fancywork produced a plethora of knick-knacks and superfluous furnishings for the Victorian home that are a distinguishing relic of Victorian taste. Articles ranged from crocheted antimacassars and doilies, beaded pincushions and watchpockets, handkerchief sachets and shaving cases, to the ubiquitous Berlin woolwork adorning everything from cushions to firescreens to the head of the family's slippers.

Being non-essential, this type of work was indicative of a genteel life, a life free from drudgery. The household's females were still usefully 'employed', though not for anything as vulgar as money. Instead, the 'gains' came through the creation of a comfortable home for their families, furnished with the results of decorative feminine industry. Or the 'gains' were philanthropic, the fancywork being sold at fashionable bazaars, a socially acceptable way of raising money for charitable causes. This type of needlework activity also gave women legitimate and worthwhile reasons to seek out each other's company. These gatherings were for such good purpose that no one could consider the occasions an excuse for idle chatter. They also provided important social contact for women who might otherwise lead lonely lives. This is probably the closest Australian women came to the North American women's quilting bees, traditional events for the co-operative making of a household's very necessary quilt supplies.

The myriad journals and magazines widely circulated during the later part of the nineteenth century flourished on the fads and fashions of fancywork. Each issue detailed new novelties to make, many of them destined to give comfort and possibly dubious pleasure to the wearer, who was invariably the head of the household. One magazine offered a 'German Plaid Comforter, Darned Necktie, Nepaulese smoking cap, shaving book, Shield-design Cigar case'.

Amongst all the bright colours, elaborate designs and often peculiar shapes of Victorian fancywork, there continued a tradition of embroidery that was subtle, refined and effective. Whitework is, as the name implies, embroidery in white thread on white fabric. The term can also include plain sewing necessary to construct garments and other home-sewn items.

From the earliest days of the colony, whitework was used principally to embellish the muslin used for women's, babies' and young children's dresses. The favoured techniques were tambouring, in which the design is worked in a series of chain stitches using a fine hook, and Ayrshire work, named after the district in Scotland in which it originated, in which the embroidered design, worked in satin and beading stitch, is further embellished by a variety of open needlework fillings worked in a fine thread. Embroidered lengths of muslin were imported from India and Britain, or skilled needlewomen made whitework either for themselves or, if less well-off, to earn money. Generally, women embroidered their own babies' clothes, especially the christening robe, which was to be used by successive generations. The use of Ayrshire work

for these continued throughout the nineteenth century.

In the mid-nineteenth century, broderie anglaise became a popular form of whitework. This is a coarser form of Ayrshire work, without the needlework filling but with the holes. The design consists of a series of holes with tightly overcast edges, the design carried between the holes in padded satin stitch and stem stitch. Broderie anglaise is worked on cotton using a soft, mercerised cotton thread. It was much used on children's dresses, women's separate sleeves and collars, and on their underclothing, particularly drawers and petticoats. As it was relatively easy to do, if time-consuming, broderie anglaise was often worked at home, though it was also possible to purchase ready-made lengths, handmade or, later in the century, machine-made.

This volume presents some of the favourite needlework styles of the Victorian era: ribbonwork, beadwork, lacemaking, crochet and whitework. Some of these continued to be popular well into the twentieth century, while others have enjoyed a more recent revival.

The selection of works in this book has been made with several aims in mind. First, it should represent, though not define, an aspect of the history of needlework in Australia. Second, works were chosen that were visually engaging, if not arresting, so that today's needleworkers might be inspired to work or to adapt the patterns. Third, works were considered in terms of the skill required to make them. It is intended that beginners as well as experts will find patterns they can accomplish and enjoy. Finally, though, the overall intent was to make available a fraction of Australia's unique needlework heritage so that contemporary makers might be informed, inspired and encouraged by the achievements of Australian women over the last two hundred years.

Ribbon Embroidery

*D*uring the past 250 years ribbon embroidery has been in fashion at various times. One has only to look at seventeenth and eighteenth century portraits of the aristocratic and well-to-do to see the extravagant use of ribbons on costume for both men and women. Ribbon bows, rosettes and ruchings abound on bodices, stomachers, robings, sleeves, hats and shoes.

Charles Germain de Saint Aubin, in his book *Àrt de Brodeur,* published in 1770, mentions backgrounds embroidered with heavy ribbon, and examples of men's waistcoats with ribbon appliqué exist in museums. The delicate, small-flowered designs usually associated with ribbon embroidery appeared on smaller items such as stomachers, pocketbooks, needlecases, pincushions, and bags.

Small bags for ladies came into use at the end of the eighteenth century, when fashionable dress, with its slender silhouette, could not accommodate the pockets, worn under the outer garments, that had previously been the method of carrying around a lady's bits and pieces. These new bags, called indispensables or reticules, were often embellished with embroidery in silk and ribbon.

In the eighteenth and early nineteenth centuries pincushions were a necessity, as pins were quite expensive, and many were made as gifts for relatives and friends. These were sometimes embellished with ribbon embroidery, and a delightful example is on display at Old Government House, Parramatta. It is a cream satin, heart-shaped cushion, embroidered with pink ribbon flowers and green leaves. It was made at the turn of the eighteenth and nineteenth centuries.

Ribbon embroidery was fashionable from the 1820s to the 1840s as decoration on men's waistcoats, women's reticules, needlecases, pincushions and other domestic items. At this time the ribbon used for embroidery was known as China ribbon. It came in a variety of colours, both plain and shaded and was about one-eighth of an inch (3 millimetres) wide.

The designs for ribbon embroidery were invariably floral and were worked mostly in straight stitches or with the ribbon gathered into circular flowers. It is rare to find an embroidery stitch worked in ribbon before the end of the nineteenth century. A chain stitch was occasionally used. A very handsome blotter cover in the Victoria and Albert Museum, London, has a design that includes roses, daisies, small flowers like forget-me-nots, wheat ears and leaves. Many of the flowers are gathered ribbon, other flowers and the leaves are worked in straight stitches. In America, samplers were worked in Pennsylvania between about 1820 and 1840 with quilled ribbon borders. Quilling was pleated, braided or gathered ribbon used for trimming. No doubt this type of trimming was used on domestic items elsewhere.

By the middle of the nineteenth century ribbon had reached a peak in design and manufacture in England and France. The beautiful floral and picture ribbons manufactured at Coventry at this time are a notable example. Yet embroidery with ribbon declined until the end of the nineteenth century, when the narrow silk ribbons became available again.

The *Needlecraft Practical Journal on Ribbonwork,* published at the beginning of the twentieth century, gives a list of ribbons available, which were introduced by William Briggs & Co. Ltd, a well-known purveyor of embroidery and lace supplies. Pompadour ribbon is described as being the one most like those that had been used in years gone by; it was about one-eighth of an inch (3 millimetres) wide and came in a great variety of colours, both plain and shaded. This ribbon was ideal for working small sprays of flowers. Giant crêpe ribbon, with a slightly crinkled surface, was excellent for larger flowers, such as poppies. This ribbon was a recent innovation at the time. Picotee ribbon was five-eighths of an inch (16 millimetres) wide, with a fine serrated edge on one side only. It was meant to be gathered along the plain edge. Its range of colours was limited to white, yellow, pale pink and full pink, each with a ruby edge, as well as shaded pink and shaded yellow. This ribbon made very realistic picotees or pinks, as the photograph on the cover of that issue of the *Needlecraft Journal* demonstrates.

During the early part of this century, catalogues from department stores in Australia regularly featured stamped designs and transfers for embroidery, including ribbonwork, or Rococco work, as it was sometimes called. Anthony Horderns' Price List for Art Needlework for June 1910 lists Pompadour ribbon, shaded and plain at sixpence a dozen yards; giant crêpe at one penny three farthings yard, or one shilling and eightpence a dozen; picotee ribbon, shaded and plain at threepence ha'penny a yard or three shillings and threepence a dozen. Also listed is cigar ribbon, both shaded and plain, at a penny a yard or tenpence a dozen.

These ribbons could be used for embroidery on mats, teacosies, bags, sachets, pillow shams, cushions and pictures. White or cream satin was a popular choice of background fabric and many items worked on this rather impractical background have survived and are now in collections in museums and the Embroiderers Guilds.

Traced designs for ribbon embroidery were sold with the design stamped on the fabric and part of the design worked as an example. The ribbons to be used were contained in a muslin pouch attached to the article. Weldons also produced a fourteen page booklet on ribbon embroidery at this time, with instructions for working floral motifs.

In the 1920s ribbon embroidery was still popular and directions for working it on clothing, underwear and children's wear appeared in magazines and specialist booklets. *Ribbon Art,* published in the United States, was being sold at Farmers in Sydney for one shilling and threepence (25 cents in the United States). Its fifty pages are packed with ideas for using ribbon on just about everything from headbands to lampshades. And *Good Needlework,* an English publication, in November 1934, gave instructions for an evening bag embroidered with ribbon couched in a circular pattern.

During the Second World War, however, suitable ribbon for embroidery became unavailable, and it was not until the 1980s that the technique of ribbon embroidery was revived. The great variety of ribbons produced today gives this type of work great scope. Fine silk ribbons are again available and make it possible to work the delicate floral designs of the past. The use of embroidery stitches in ribbon is more prevalent today than it has ever been. Hand stitchery in a combination of ribbons and threads makes a very rich texture and can be worked effectively on clothing, bags, boxes, cushions, jewellery and pictures.

Detail of table centre
c. 1910 Australian
Designer unknown, embroidered by
Mrs Corbett, in Sydney
Silk satin, silk ribbons and silk
thread, silk cord
79 x 53 centimetres
Embroiderers Guild New South Wales,
Inc., Sydney

The table centre is of cream silk satin with a design at each end of a basket of roses and small flowers, suspended by a ribbon bow. Trails of small flowers connect this part of the design to a circular garland of roses and a bow at each side. The roses are padded and worked with straight stitches in silk ribbon in shades of pink. The small pale pink and blue flowers are worked in silk ribbon, either gathered into a circle or in straight stitches. The leaves are worked in green silk ribbon in small straight stitches. Stems are worked in stem stitch in olive green silk thread. The bow is in satin stitch in pale blue silk thread. The roses at the sides are formed with loops of shaded silk gauze ribbon, two loops to each of the five petals. The centres are worked in yellow silk thread in french knots. A cream silk cord, knotted at intervals, is sewn to the edge of the embroidered centre, with a frill of pale blue silk edged with pink shaded ribbon. The table centre is lined with silk.

Photograph Peter Henning

RIBBON EMBROIDERY TECHNIQUE

For ribbon embroidery, it is best to use a chenille needle, which has a large eye and a sharp point. If a chenille needle is not available, use a tapestry needle, which has a large eye and a blunt point. When sewing with fine silk ribbon, a crewel needle of suitable size is adequate.

If you have difficulty pulling the ribbon through the fabric, gently pierce the fabric with the tip of a stiletto without breaking the fabric threads.

Always make stitches in ribbon a little looser than usual, to let the ribbon fluff out and sit softly on the fabric.

Leave ends about 1 centimetre long when starting and finishing ribbons. Sew these down with sewing cotton when a section of the work is completed.

Motif for handkerchief bag (actual size) on page 9

To transfer designs to fabric

First trace the design onto tissue paper with a hard sharp pencil. Only the main lines of the design are necessary, not every small flower and leaf. These are easily followed from the photographs or patterns for the motifs. Pin the traced design into place on the fabric. Sew along the lines of the design with sewing cotton in a small running stitch through both paper and fabric. Tear away the tissue paper, leaving the design outlined in running stitch. Use light-coloured sewing cotton on dark fabrics and a colour that will show up well on light fabrics, though you should avoid using too dark a colour, in case there is any transfer of dye.

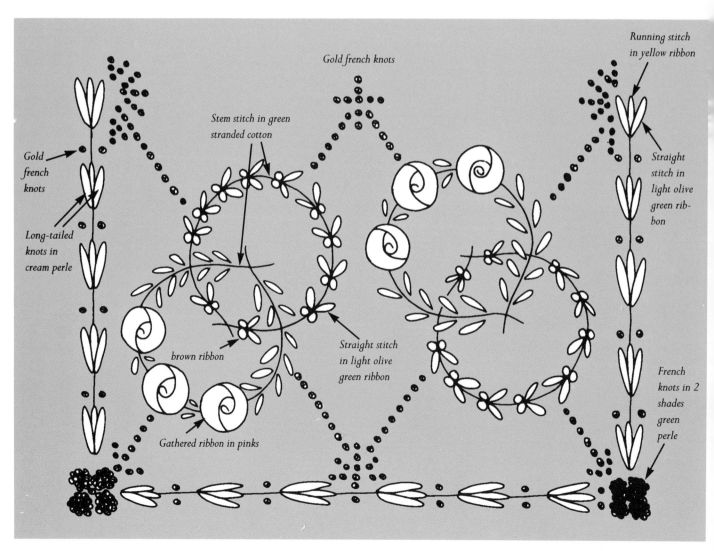

Gold french knots

Running stitch in yellow ribbon

Stem stitch in green stranded cotton

Gold french knots

Straight stitch in light olive green ribbon

Long-tailed knots in cream perle

brown ribbon

Straight stitch in light olive green ribbon

Gathered ribbon in pinks

French knots in 2 shades green perle

Heather Joynes

HANDKERCHIEF BAG

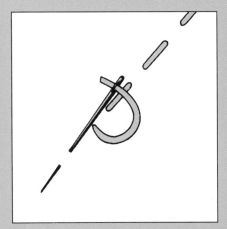

Running stitch

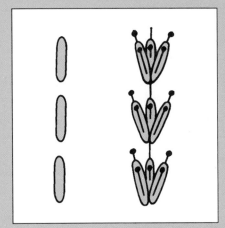

Floral border

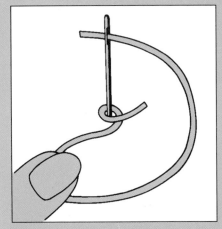

Long-tailed knot

The instructions here are designed for you to duplicate the bag as it appears in the photograph on page 17, but the embroidery pattern could also be used on a shorter hand-kerchief bag or sachet.

Finished size

34 x 21 centimetres

Materials

❖ 40 centimetres of 90 centimetre wide firm cream satin
❖ 40 centimetres of 90 centimetre wide cream lining
❖ 2 metres each of 3 millimetre wide silk ribbon in three shades of pink
❖ 2 metres of 3 millimetre wide silk ribbon in yellow
❖ 3 metres of 3 millimetre wide silk ribbon in olive green
❖ 2 metres of 3 millimetre wide silk ribbon in light olive green
❖ 2 metres of 3 millimetre wide silk ribbon in light brown
❖ DMC perle cotton no. 8 in the following colours:
      Ecru
    470 Green
    471 Green
❖ DMC stranded cotton in green no. 471
❖ Gold thread, Madeira metallic no. 15
❖ 1.5 metres of cream cord
❖ No. 6 crewel needle to use with ribbons, perle and gold threads
❖ No. 8 crewel needle to use with stranded cotton
❖ Machine sewing cotton to match fabric

Method

Cut two pieces of cream satin 36 x 23 centi-metres. This includes a 1 centimetre seam allowance all round. Transfer the main lines of the design to one piece of the satin, using the

*Detail of handkerchief bag
Date unknown Probably English
Designer and embroiderer unknown
Silk satin, silk ribbons and threads,
sequins, gold metal thread
34 x 21 centimetres
Museum of Applied Arts and Sciences,
Sydney*

The bag is of cream silk satin with a design of wreaths of pink flowers and brown berries and green leaves embroidered in silk ribbons and threads. The border around three sides has been worked in yellow and green ribbons and thread; small sequins dec-orate the end of each flower. A dia-pered background is worked in french knots in gold metal thread, which has tarnished. The bag is hand-sewn, with a casing at the top, and faced with pink fabric. The casing is threaded with cream cord.

Photograph Penelope Clay

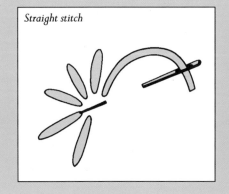

Straight stitch

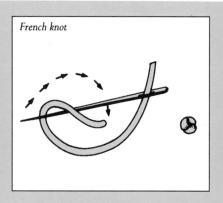

French knot

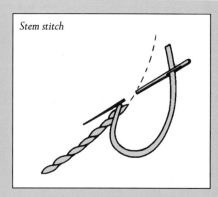

Stem stitch

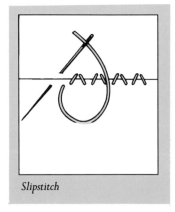

Slipstitch

method described on page 8.

The border Start the embroidery with the border. Make a row of running stitches in the yellow ribbon along the line of the border flowers. The running stitches should be 1.5 centimetres long and 5 millimetres apart.

Work a long-tailed knot over the centre of each running stitch in the cream perle cotton.

Work a straight stitch on each side of the running stitches in olive green ribbon, then a long-tailed knot in the lighter green perle cotton over each of these stitches.

Add three straight stitches in green perle cotton number 470 at the top of each flower. Work a french knot in gold thread at the end of the two outer stitches; this replaces the tiny sequins in the original.

Work four clusters of french knots at the lower corners of the border, using perle cotton in the two greens, making the centres of each cluster dark green surrounded by the light green.

Flowers The pink flowers are made by gathering the silk ribbon along one edge by whipping over the edge and pulling up the thread to gather the ribbon into a small circle. This is better than a running stitch to gather the ribbon. The centre flower is worked with the deepest pink outside and mid-pink in the centre. The other two flowers have light pink in the centre and mid-pink outside.

Stems and leaves Work the stems in stem stitch in one thread of green stranded cotton number 471. Work the leaves in straight stitches with the light olive green ribbon.

Berries and lines Work the berries in the other wreath with brown ribbon in french knots. The stems and leaves are worked in the same way as for the first wreath.

Work the lines of french knots in gold thread on the diamond pattern and at the points of the diamonds.

Finishing

Press the work carefully on the wrong side, with the embroidery face down on a well-padded surface, such as a soft towel.

With the right sides together, stitch the two halves of the bag together to 17 centimetres from the top. Hand or machine stitching can be used.

Cut the lining the same as the bag and seam in the same way, taking in a fraction more seam. Insert the lining into the bag. Turn under the seam allowance on both the outside and the lining and slipstitch at the sides 2 centimetres from the top, and across the top. Work two rows of stitching across the top, just inside the edge, and 2 centimetres below the edge to form a casing.

Cut the cord in half and thread each piece through the casing. Knot the ends together.

Heather Joynes

VICTORIAN EVENING BAG

Finished size

24 x 22 centimetres

Materials

- ❖ 40 centimetres of 90 centimetre wide firm black satin
- ❖ 20 centimetres of 90 centimetre wide black lining
- ❖ 2 metres of 3 millimetre wide silk ribbon in red
- ❖ 1 metre of 3 millimetre wide silke ribbon in purple
- ❖ 6 metres of 3 millimetre wide silk ribbon in yellow
- ❖ 6 metres of 3 millimetre wide silk ribbon in white
- ❖ 8 metres of 3 millimetre wide silk ribbon in olive green
- ❖ 1 metre of 3 millimetre wide silk ribbon in emerald green
- ❖ DMC stranded cotton in the following colours:
  699 Green
  962 Pink
- ❖ 2 metres of 2 centimetres wide black satin ribbon
- ❖ 50 centimetres of 3 centimetre wide black silky fringe
- ❖ No. 6 crewel needle to use with the silk ribbon
- ❖ No. 8 crewel needle to use with stranded cotton
- ❖ Black machine sewing cotton

Method

Enlarge the pattern for the bag. From the black satin cut out the two sides of the bag using the pattern (page 13). Transfer the main lines of the design to the satin by tacking through tissue paper with white cotton, as described on page 8.
Fuchsias Start the embroidery with the fuchsias. Make two straight stitches in purple silk

The instructions here describe how to make this Victorian black silk evening bag as it appears in the photograph. Individual motifs or all of its floral decoration could also be used to embellish modern bag or purse styles.

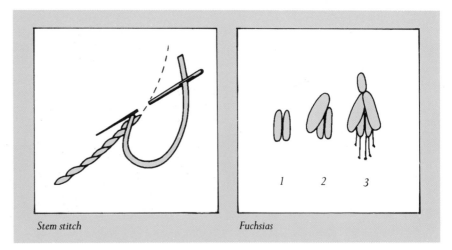

Stem stitch   Fuchsias

Illustrated in colour on page 18.

ribbon, then work two straight stitches over these in red ribbon and another small straight stitch at the top to form a calyx. Work the stamens in stem stitch, using one strand of pink stranded cotton number 962. Work three satin stitches at the end of each stamen in the same thread. Work the stems in stem stitch in one strand of emerald green stranded cotton, number 699. Work the leaves in small straight stitches in emerald green ribbon. Work the buds with a straight stitch in red ribbon.

Yellow flowers These are worked in five small straight stitches in a circle, with a small straight stitch at the centre in white. Work the stems in stem stitch in one strand of green stranded cotton number 699. Using the olive green ribbon, work the leaves in small straight stitches.

Borders Work the white flowers with five straight stitches for the petals and a small straight stitch in yellow for the centres. The buds are worked in white ribbon in small straight stitches. The stems are worked in one strand of green stranded cotton number 699,

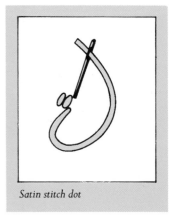

Satin stitch dot

Motif for bag (actual size)

Yellow flowers

and the leaves in small straight stitches in olive green ribbon.

The back of the bag Repeat the embroidery on the reverse side of the bag, using white for the fuchsias and small flowers in the centre. The flowers in the border are worked in yellow, with white centres.

Finishing

Press the work carefully on the wrong side, with the embroidery face down on a well-padded surface, such as a soft towel.

Place the front and back pieces of the bag right sides together, and stitch the sides together to under the line of the drawstring casing.

Work by hand or machine.

Cut two piecs of lining the same as the lower part of the bag, that is from the top line of the casing. Sew these two pieces together, taking in a fraction more seam than on the main pieces of the bag. Insert the lining into the bag and pin or tack bag and lining together at the upper casing line.

Fold the top of the bag to the inside at the fold line, and hem over the lining at the lower casing line. Slipstitch the heading to the upper casing line. Stitch along the two casing lines.

Sew the fringe to the edge of the bag.

Cut the length of black satin ribbon in half and thread each piece through the casing. Tie the ends in a bow and stitch to secure.

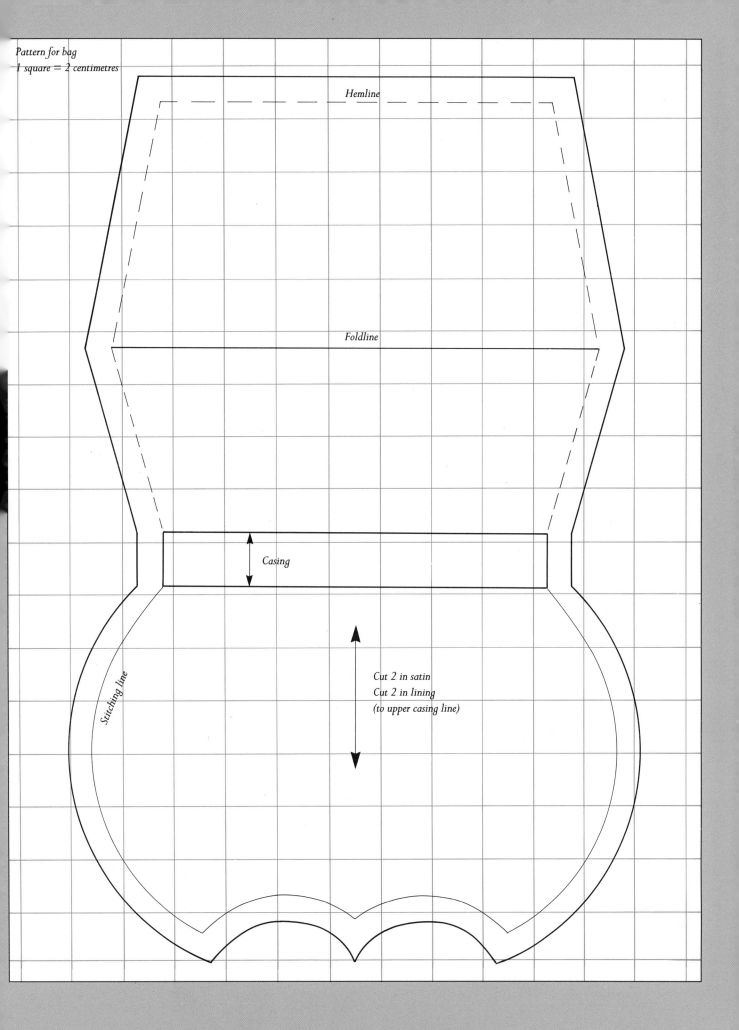

Pattern for bag
1 square = 2 centimetres

Hemline

Foldline

Casing

Stitching line

Cut 2 in satin
Cut 2 in lining
(to upper casing line)

BASKET AND BOWS TABLE CENTRE

Heather Joyne

*T*he delicate work on this table centre could be copied onto a similar piece, or motifs from the design—the bows, garlands, trails of flowers or the basket—could be worked on other articles, such as sachets, lingerie or hosiery bags.

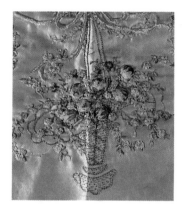

Detail of table centre
c. 1910 Australian
Designer unknown, embroidered by
Mrs Corbett, in Sydney
Silk satin, silk ribbons and silk
thread, silk cord
79 x 53 centimetres
Embroiderers Guild New South
Wales, Inc., Sydney

Photograph Peter Henning
Illustrated in colour on page 27

Finished size

79 x 53 centimetres

Materials

- ❖ 70 x 42 centimetre piece of cream satin
- ❖ 1 metre of cream silk for the lining and frill
- ❖ 6 metres each of 3 millimetre wide silk ribbon in three shades of pink
- ❖ 6 metres each of 3 millimetre wide silk ribbon in pale pink and pale blue
- ❖ 4 metres each of 3 millimetre wide silk ribbon in two shades of olive green
- ❖ 4 metres each of 1 centimetre wide silk or soft nylon ribbon in four shades of pink
- ❖ 2 metres of silk or soft nylon ribbon in pale yellow
- ❖ 5 metres of 1 centimetre wide silk or soft nylon ribbon in pale pink, for the frill
- ❖ DMC perle 8 cotton in the following colours:
  - 747 Pale blue
  - 963 Pale pink
- ❖ DMC stranded cotton in the following colours:
  - 436 Tan
  - 471 Green
  - 743 Yellow
- ❖ No. 18 chenille needle to use with the 1 centimetre ribbon
- ❖ No. 6 crewel needle to use with the 3 millimetre ribbon and perle cotton 8 cotton
- ❖ No. 8 crewel needle to use with stranded cotton
- ❖ 3.5 metres of cream cord

Method

Enlarge the design by using the enlarger on a photocopier or by using the grid to scale up the design. Transfer the design onto the satin, using the method described on page 8. Note that only the large flowers have been marked on the pattern. The leaves and small flowers can be used to fill the spaces between the main flowers.

The basket Using one strand of tan stranded cotton number 436, work chain stitch around the outline of the basket, then running stitch in fine lines across the basket, following the curve in the base of the basket. While your running stitches should be fairly regular in size, don't line up the stitches in each row, as more random placement will give a better basketweave effect.

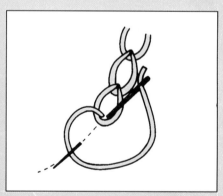

Chain stitch

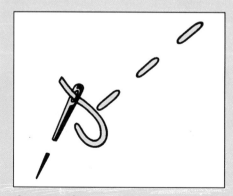

Running stitch

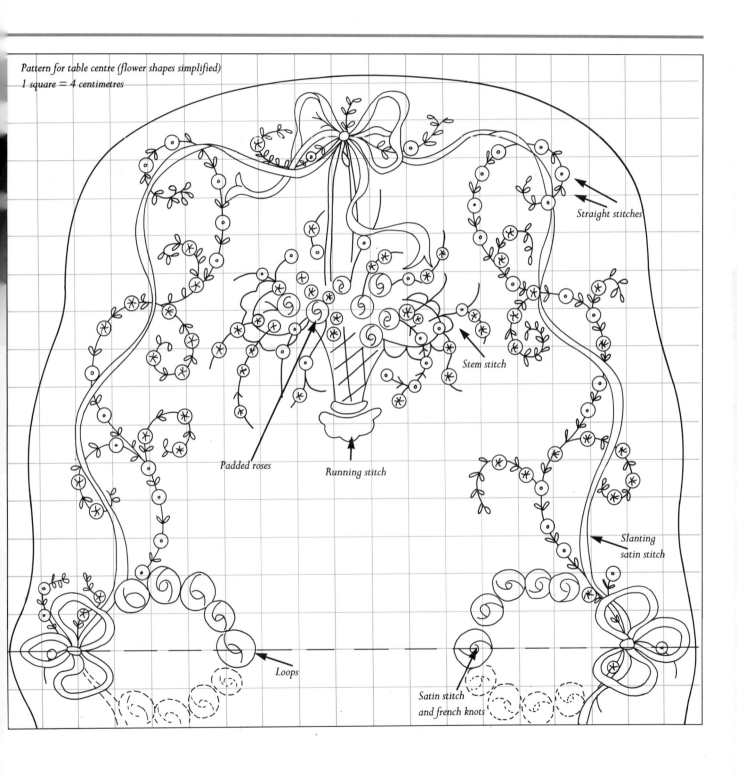

Pattern for table centre (flower shapes simplified)
1 square = 4 centimetres

Straight stitches

Stem stitch

Padded roses

Running stitch

Slanting satin stitch

Loops

Satin stitch and french knots

Roses To work the full-blown roses, first work two blocks of three satin stitches, one over the other, using pink perle 8 cotton, number 963 (1). This forms the padding for the roses. Now, with the deepest pink 3 milli-metre ribbon, work three straight stitches over the centre of the padding (2,3). Continue in a similar way with the other shades of pink ribbon until the padding is completely covered and the rose formed (4). Work from the darkest to the lightest pink.

The roses in profile are worked over satin stitch padding, as for the full-blown roses (1). Make overlapping straight stitches over the padding, using ribbon in the two deepest pinks (2,3). Add five or six stitches in the lightest pink ribbon from the base of the padded section (4).

Other flowers The small pink and blue flowers are made with either five small straight stitches into a central point or a gathered circle of ribbon. To gather the ribbon, whip over the edge to be gathered, and draw up the thread so the ribbon forms a circle. This is better than a running stitch. The centres of flowers made with straight stitches are made with a single french knot worked in two strands of yellow stranded cotton.

Trails of flowers Work along the stem lines in stem stitch in one strand of green stranded cotton number 471. Then work the small flowers in pink and blue 3 millimetre ribbon, in five straight stitches or as gathered circles. Then work the leaves in 3 millimetre green ribbon, using both shades randomly.

Ribbon and bow Work these in slanting satin stitch in pale blue perle 8 cotton number 477.

Rose garlands The deepest colour in the garland is at the lower part, so start with the central rose. Make two loops of 1 centimetre ribbon in the two deeper shades of pink for each of the five petals. The loops sit softly on

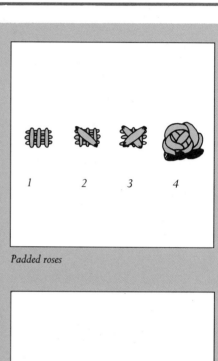

Padded roses

Profile roses

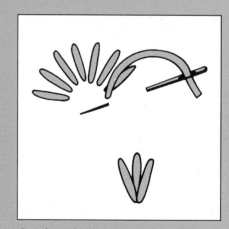

Straight stitch

Handkerchief bag
Date unknown Probably English
Designer and embroiderer unknown
Silk satin, silk ribbons and threads, sequins, gold metal thread
34 x 21 centimetres
Museum of Applied Arts and Sciences, Sydney

The bag is of cream silk satin with a design of wreaths of pink flowers and brown berries and green leaves embroidered in silk ribbons and threads. The border around three sides has been worked in yellow and green ribbons and thread; small sequins decorate the end of each flower. A diapered background is worked in french knots in gold metal thread, which has tarnished. The bag is hand-sewn, with a casing at the top, and faced with pink fabric. The casing is threaded with cream cord.
This bag looks as if it could be an early nineteenth century piece that has been reworked, perhaps in the 1930s. The very fine hand-sewing, the use of metal thread and the style of the design all suggest a date in the early 1800s, and the tiny sequins used are likely to date before 1850. It could have been a reticule or indispensable, which the bag's long shape would have suited, but it has been remade into an unusually long handkerchief bag. There are also traces of previous sewing on the upper half of the bag, while the cord and sewing at the top of the bag do not match the fine work of the embroidery.

Photograph Penelope Clay

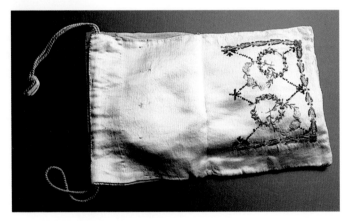

Chrysanthemum panel
c. 1900
Origin and embroiderer unknown, signed 'Vera'
Velvet, with rayon and silk ribbons
38 x 30 centimetres
Embroiderer's Guild New South Wales, Inc., Sydney

The background of the panel is black velvet. The chrysanthemums are worked in rayon ribbon, twisted to form curled petals. The sepals of the flowers and buds in profile are of silk ribbon in straight stitches. The chrysanthemums have been painted after being worked to achieve the beautiful shaded colouring. The stems are formed with twisted silk ribbon. The heaviest stem has been made by twisting the ribbon around the threads of a soft cotton cord. The leaves are made with long straight stitches of wide silk ribbon sewn down with straight stitches. The panel is signed 'Vera' in yellow paint in the lower right-hand corner. It is a very unusual piece, and very accomplished. 'Vera' was obviously a master of the technique. This is the only piece of its kind I have ever seen.

Photograph Peter Henning

Drawstring bag
c. 1850 English
Designer and embroiderer unknown
Silk satin, silk ribbon, silk thread and silk cord fringe
24 x 22 centimetres
Museum of Applied Arts and Sciences, Sydney

The drawstring bag is made of black satin, embroidered with silk ribbons and silk thread. On each side of the bag a spray of fuchsias and small flowers is surrounded by a border on three sides of flowers and leaves. On one side the fuchsias are red and purple with yellow flowers in the centre, and white flowers in the border. The other side has white fuchsias and white flowers in the centre, and yellow flowers in the border. A black silk fringe decorates the lower part of the bag, and the casing is threaded with silk ribbon.

Photograph Penelope Clay

French knots

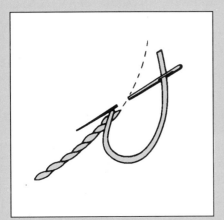

Stem stitch

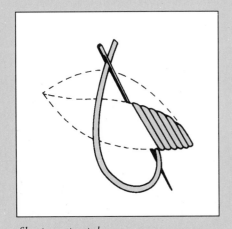

Slanting satin stitch

the fabric.

Work the other roses to each side of this rose in graduating shades of pink, using pink and yellow for the top, and lightest, flowers. Each rose has three or four satin stitches at the centre, worked in two strands of green stranded cotton, surrounded by five or six french knots worked in four strands of yellow stranded cotton number 743. (Because the ribbon used in the original is not available now the roses may not look exactly like the originals and it may be necessary to sew the petals down here and there with matching sewing cotton.)

The leaves around these roses are worked in stem stitch in one strand of green stranded cotton number 471.

Finishing

Cut the embroidered satin to the shape of the centre, allowing 1 centimetre turnings. Cut a piece of lining silk the same as the top of the table centre.

Cut four 7 centimetre wide pieces across the fabric width of lining for the frill. Join these together by hand or machine and turn up and stitch a narrow hem on one edge. Sew pale pink ribbon over the hem. Gather the frill to fit around the table centre. Tack the frill to the edge of the table centre, right sides together.

Pin the lining over the worked centre, right sides together, and then sew together. Leave an opening of about 10 centimetres on one side to turn the work to the right side. Turn right side out and press carefully from the back, with the embroidery face down into a soft towel. Slipstitch the opening closed.

Sew the cream cord, knotted at intervals if you wish, over the join of the edge and the frill.

CHRYSANTHEMUM PANEL

Heather Joyne

he chrysanthemums on this panel can be worked either in two shades of ribbon that are then painted with dye after being worked, which the original embroiderer used, or in several shades of ribbon. It is essential that soft ribbon is used. Soft nylon or, if obtainable, rayon ribbon is best. Satin ribbon is not suitable.

Detail of chrysanthemum panel
c. 1900
Origin and embroiderer unknown,
signed 'Vera'
Velvet, with rayon and silk ribbons
38 x 30 centimetres
Embroiderer's Guild New South
Wales, Inc., Sydney

Photograph Peter Henning
Illustrated in colour on page 17

Finished size

38 x 30 centimetres

Materials

❖ 35 x 40 centimetre piece of black velvet or velveteen
❖ 20 centimetres of piping cord
❖ No. 18 chenille needle
❖ A stiletto or awl
❖ A scrap of wadding (for large flower centre)
❖ Machine sewing cotton to match the green ribbon
❖ If the panel is worked in several shades, you will need:
❖ 3 metres each of two close shades of 1 centimetre wide ribbon in pale yellow and soft orange
❖ 2 metres of two close shades of 1 centimetre wide mauve ribbon

❖ 2 metres of 1 centimetre wide pale green ribbon
❖ 4 metres of 1 centimetre wide silk ribbon in soft green
❖ 2 metres of 3 millimetre wide silk ribbon in a matching green
❖ If the ribbon is to be painted after working, you will need the same quantities of green ribbons and
❖ 8 metres of 1 centimetre wide pale yellow ribbon
❖ 4 metres of 1 centimetre wide pale mauve ribbon
❖ Fabric dye that can be diluted in water in pale green, orange and mauve
❖ Small artist's brush

Method

Enlarge the pattern using the enlarger on a photocopier or scale up using the grid system (see the general instructions in chapter 6). Transfer the design to the black velvet by the method described on page 8. Note that only the broad outlines of the pattern in which the stitches are to be worked are given. Start the embroidery with the stems and then leaves, and work the flowers last.

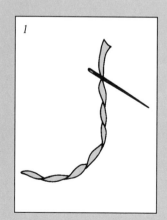

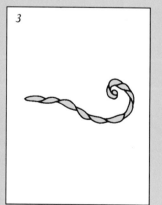

Ribbon twist

Motif for chrysanthemum panel
square = 2 centimetres

Stems For the main stem, take about 15 centimetres of piping cord and unravel it. Wind green ribbon around all the strands, starting 3 centimetres from one end. When 5 centimetres of the cord are covered, divide the strands into two and wind these with the ribbon. Leave at least 3 centimetres of cord at the end. Thread each strand of cord into a large needle and take them through the velvet at the ends of the stem. If necessary pierce a hole with a stiletto or awl. Sew the stem to the velvet as invisibly as possible.

The smaller stems are made by winding the ribbon around one strand of the piping cord and then it taking through the velvet in the same way.

The stems of the buds are twisted ribbon sewn to the velvet.

Leaves Work the leaves by making several long, rather loose, straight stitches in the 1 centimetre wide green silk ribbon. Then make a series of straight stitches with the 3 millimetre green ribbon, working them down the long straight stitches, as in the original piece.

Flowers Each petal of the chrysanthemums is made by bringing the ribbon through the velvet, twisting it, making a small curl at the end of the petal, which is held down with the left thumb while the needle is put into the centre of the curl, and gently pulling the needle and ribbon through to the back of the work. This takes a little practice, so it would be a good idea to work a test piece on a scrap of velvet before you start.

Each petal must be made separately, cutting the ends of the ribbon when the petal is finished, and leaving tags of ribbon at the back to be sewn down later. Otherwise the work will become puckered. When several petals have been completed, sew down the ends of the ribbon at the back of the work with machine sewing cotton. If you are using sev-

eral shades of ribbon for the flowers, work the different shades around the flower in a similar way to the original.

Start on the largest flower in the centre of the lower section of petals. The petals at the back of this flower are worked in straight stitches, with the ribbon twisted.

To make the raised centre of the largest chrysanthemum, form a small ring with a scrap of wadding and sew this in place at the centre of the flower with a few stitches over the ring. Work straight stitches in ribbon over the ring, bringing the needle through the fabric on the outside of the ring and down into the centre. Continue in this way until the centre is full and raised.

Work the mauve flower next, in the same way, omitting the raised centre. Then work the profile flowers, working the petals first, then the sepals in green silk ribbon with straight stitches, taking them in between the petals. Work the buds in the same way.

If you are going to paint the worked flowers with dye, mix the desired colours and test them on a spare piece of ribbon. Let the ribbon dry, as the dye will dry a little lighter, so you can see what the final colour will be. The dye should run into the ribbon to give a soft effect. It may be necessary to damp the worked flowers slightly before applying the dye. Paint the dye onto the worked flowers carefully, starting with the pale green at the centres.

Finishing

When finished, the panel should be stretched over acid-free cardboard and either laced or glued to the back (see chapter 6 for directions), then framed, unglazed, in a suitable frame.

Beadwork

As early as 1832 the Sydney merchants Messrs Lamb, Buchanan and Co. were advertising 'beads of colours', amongst the items for sale in a recently arrived shipload of household goods.[1] Annie Walker, recalling her childhood in New South Wales during the 1830s and 1840s, listed beadwork amongst the fancywork styles fashionable at the time,[2] and throughout the nineteenth century, women's magazines published detailed instructions for making a wide variety of beadwork projects suitable for decorating the home and person. The Victorian interior was swagged, stuffed, upholstered and fringed to the point of suffocation, and the richness afforded to household furnishings by beaded embellishment was much admired.

The luxuriance of beaded embroidery has ensured the preservation of many examples of this craft, their survival enhanced by the brilliant colour of the beads, which do not fade on prolonged exposure to light as textiles do. The main threat to the condition of beaded artefacts is the sheer weight of the beads themselves, which can stress the threads and fabrics to which they are attached, even to the point of disintegration.

The use of beads in embroidery can involve the entire design being worked in beads on a thread or fabric base or the addition of beaded elements to designs, worked in amongst other types of embroidery. Beads can also be made into tasselled or fringed edgings. Suitable beads for Victorian embroidery are those made of porcelain, glass and metal; in past centuries beads were also available in semi-precious varieties, made from amber, coral, rock crystal, jade, turquoise and jet.

An important task to be completed before beginning any beaded fancywork project involved sorting the beads, by size and colour, and storing each group, for easy access, in the small containers often still found in old work-boxes and worktables. A long, fine needle and a small lump of beeswax were the other pieces of specialised equipment required for this technique: the wax was used to coat the sewing thread to help the beads slide along as well to strengthen the thread and prevent knotting.

Three main varieties of bead embroidery were popular in the nineteenth century, each with its own distinctive style. Beads were sewn onto canvas, using the intricately patterned designs intended for woolwork embroidery, to produce fire and candle screens, vase and lamp mats, cushion covers and shelf trimmings—to name just a few of the surfaces covered in this way. The beads were stitched down separately across the squares of the canvas and each bead represented a stitch on the chart. This technique was often combined with woolwork to give highlights to areas of the design. Glass beads lent a luminous quality to the canvaswork, while metallic beading added richness. (Beadwork on canvas is featured in *Cross stitch, Counted Thread and Canvaswork* in the Australian Heritage Needlework series).

Another type of beadwork was also worked in this manner on canvas, but it exclusively used white, grey and black beads, both transparent and opaque. Known as 'grisaille' work, this technique relied on the contrast between light and dark, and the shades in between to give motifs the appearance of carved stone. Grisaille work was often combined with woolwork, but it could also be used to decorate silk plush and satin.

The Victorian preoccupation with afternoon tea produced one of the greatest landmarks of needlework in this period, the embroidered teacosy. These, often huge, hemispherical targets for the needleworker's art dominated the table, in pride of place in the middle of the parlour or drawing-room, keeping the tea piping hot inside the family's best silver or porcelain teapot. The teacosy was often deemed a suitable vehicle for the 'chef d'oeuvre' undertaken by young girls in their final year of schooling, when the finishing touches were put to their social technique. The cosies were usually made of silk plush, with a quilted lining to provide insulation, and ornamented heavily with any combination of plushwork, ribbonwork, braiding or beadwork ostentatious enough to indicate the embroiderer's status and social position, or pretensions. The example illustrated is made of blue silk velvet decorated with a central rose design surrounded by foliage and four buds, all worked in grisaille beading, attached by the 'lazy squaw method' and further embellished with artificial pearls. The term 'lazy squaw' refers to the couching of strings of beads in position, rather than sewing each bead down individually; it was a technique used by the Indian women of North America.

A similarly monochromatic effect was popular in the 1870s and 1880s when beads were used to encrust household objects like the pincushion illustrated, which was intended for storing hat pins on a lady's dressing table. This technique used transparent crystal beads, often with metallic linings, in combination with white beads to create raised, three-dimensional floral motifs, usually arranged in wreaths and surmounted by artificial pearl centres. These floral tributes were mostly worked on silk plush and trimmed with tassels or looped fringes of beads. When making beaded fringes or tassels, Victorian women did not knot between each bead, which may account for the losses suffered by most surviving examples; as once the anchor thread was broken there was nothing to prevent the beads from dropping off.

This pincushion was made to match a pair of watch pockets, the small pouches that hung on the dressing-table mirror posts and in which watches were stored when not being carried. These could also be hung over the bed, fastened onto the bed curtain. The pockets also came in larger versions, which were hung from the bed posts and were used to store items that could then be easily retrieved by the occupants of the bed.

The eighteenth century fashion for wearing decorative aprons remained popular during the nineteenth century. Usually made of impractical, unwashable silks and embroidered or embellished with ribbons or beads, these frivolous versions of the utilitarian apron were worn whilst entertaining callers in the parlour or drawing-room. They were also worn outside the home, for example, behind the sale table at fancywork bazaars held to raise funds for worthy causes. The beaded apron illustrated dates from the 1880s. Made of cotton-backed silk sateen, the skirt of this apron has a floral border worked in silver-lined crystal beads, which also trim the patch pocket and bib. The apron has no ties and would have been pinned into place. It is edged with machine-made lace.

Beadwork on costume was fashionable during the late nineteenth and early twentieth centuries, reaching a peak in the beaded dance dresses of the 1920s flappers. Beading on household objects declined in the twentieth century, the last vestige of their former glory being their use on the fly deterrent, milk jug cover.

1. *Sydney Morning Herald,* 19 March 1832, column 4.
2. Annie Walker, Family Traditions and Personal Recollections of the Family (ML MLL C195) n.d., p. 24.

June Powys

EMBROIDERY WITH BEADS

Beads Beads may be made from glass, steel, porcelain, and other materials. They may be round, oval, long, smooth or carved, transparent or opaque, in single colours or iridescent.

Equipment In addition to the beads, sequins and pearls, a good strong thread is necessary. Thread to match the bead colour is generally used, but an invisible thread may be needed in special works. Some beads are sharp and tend to cut the thread.

Beading fabric pictures To-day many printed fabrics are bold and eye-catching, and by spotting, outlining or filling on those fabrics various effects can be achieved. You may wish to pad areas of the design being highlighted with beads. If so a backing fabric is required, such as lawn. Use cotton or nylon wadding for padding, as in trapunto quilting.

When sewing beads onto a fragile fabric or on knitwear, the article will require the support of a backing fabric, such as muslin, voile, organdie or organza.

Transferring designs The design to be worked can be drawn onto tissue paper and basted in position on the right side of garment This tacking should not follow the design lines; just tack a broad grid, say along the centre vertical and horizontal lines across the two diagonals. The tacking is just to hold the paper in place. Sew the beads on through the paper, fabric and backing, then, when the beadwork is complete, gently tear the tissue away.

The design to be worked can also be drawn onto organdie, which is then basted to the right side of fabric to be decorated. The design can be worked by beading through the organdie and fabric. Then, when the project is complete, the organdie is trimmed back to the design edge.

Other all-over designs can be threadlined. Only the outline of the design should be outlined with thread.

To attach beads Most beads, pearls or shells, or bugle beads have holes through which a

Bead and sequin work is very popular for evening wear, bags, shoes, belts, buckles and buttons. It is even seen on T-shirts and jeans.

thread will run. Use a very fine beading needle. Use a backstitch to attach a bead to the fabric; each stitch should be just long enough to match the length of bead.

In some designs a number of beads can be strung together onto the thread and attached together. Bring the needle and thread up through the fabric, thread on the beads, and hold the beads closely packed together. Use a second thread that matches the fabric to couch down between each bead. Sometimes the couching is worked only after groups of beads (the 'lazy squaw' method), but this is not very secure and it is not recommended. Beads already strung can be couched onto garment.

In some work, the thread can be waxed to prevent wear and tear. Thread waxers can be bought from haberdashers, but they can also be made quite easily.

How to make a thread waxer Buy beeswax from a chemist. Place it in a saucepan on a low heat on the stove and melt. Line an egg-cup with aluminium foil and pour the melted beeswax into the foil-lined cup and allow it to cool and set. Remove the wax shape encased in foil, and this can be used as a waxer. Draw your thread across the wax several times before commencing beading work.

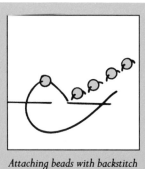

Attaching beads with backstitch

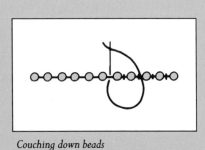

Couching down beads

The 'lazy squaw' method of couching down strings of beads

THE VAUCLUSE HOUSE PINCUSHION

June Powy

*T*his stunning pincushion was designed to hold hatpins on a dressing table, at a time when functional articles of all kinds were turned into elaborate decorative pieces.

Pincushion
c. 1860 English or Australian
Designer and maker unknown
Beads and celluloid pearls on silk velvet
16.5 x 18 centimetres
Historic Houses Trust of New South Wales, Vaucluse House

Made to ornament a lady's dressing table, pincushions like these were used to store hatpins. They often came with matching pockets for storing watches, which hung from the dressing-table mirror posts.

Photograph Peter Henning

Illustrated in colour on page 28

Finished size

18 x 18 centimetres

Materials

❖ 30 x 30 centimetre square of scarlet velvet
❖ 30 x 30 centimetre square of cotton backing fabric in matching fabric colour
❖ 30 x 30 centimetre piece of fabric for the back of the cushion
❖ Polyfill or washed lambswool or wool yarn scraps for stuffing the pincushion
❖ Small amount of polyfill for padding parts of the design
❖ No. 14 beading needle
❖ Gütermann Polytwist in white for beading
❖ Rocaille beads, 2 millimetres, in the following colours*
   281 Clear crystal
   309 Milk (or opaque)
   311/8 White
   600/11 White, small
❖ Twenty-eight 8 millimetre pearls
❖ Waxer
❖ Round-ended bodkin
❖ Tissue or tracing paper

Method

Mark the horizontal and vertical centre lines on the fabric and make a paper pattern of the pincushion shape (page 32). Pin the pattern onto the velvet, matching the centre lines of pattern with the centre lines on the velvet, and use a line of tacking to outline the pattern shape on the velvet. Mark the seam line 1.5 centimetres outside the pattern shape on the velvet. Work another tacking outline 1 cen-

timetre inside the seam line, and then another tacking line 1 centimetre inside that for the beading line. Trace the pattern for the beading design onto tracing paper and tack it in place on the velvet. Tack a fairly broad grid to hold the paper in place; you should not tack along the design lines. Bead through the paper.

The petals on the large flowers and the top of the buds appear to be padded in the style of trapunto quilting, so after tacking the tissue paper with the design on the top, tack the cotton backing fabric onto the wrong side of the velvet. Outline the parts to be padded with a very fine running stitch, working through the velvet and the backing. Cut a small slash in the backing only in the centre of each area to be padded, and use a round-ended bodkin to push stuffing or teased out wadding into the space until it is well and evenly padded. Mould each shape carefully. Stitch the slash closed with small stitches in matching thread.

Beading Read the general notes on beading on page 25. Commencing with the large flowers, attach the centre pearl, first waxing the thread, then the six outer pearls. Place loops of crystal beads between the pearl beads, with eight beads on each loop. Then work the petals of the large flowers by threading short strings of crystal beads, starting at the centre of the petal. Attach the strings from the edge of the centre of the flower to the outside edge of the petal. Use a separate thread to couch down between each bead. After completing four large flowers, then work the buds in the corner. Use the same technique as for the large flower petals, commencing with the centre of the bud. When the buds are completed, add stamens. These consist of seven crystal beads with three white 2 millimetre beads at the end.

Next, work the leaf shapes, using same technique of small strings of beads, as in the lazy squaw method, but couch down between

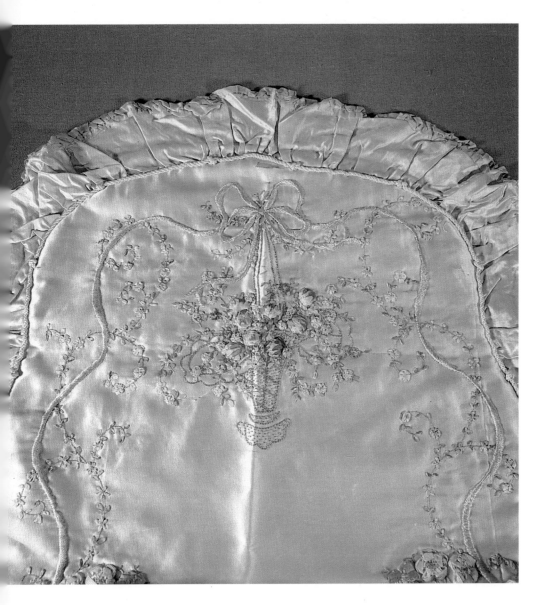

Table centre
c. 1910 Australian
Designer unknown, embroidered by
Mrs Corbett, in Sydney
Silk satin, silk ribbons and silk thread,
silk cord
79 x 53 centimetres
Embroiderers Guild New South Wales,
Inc., Sydney

The table centre is of cream silk satin with a design at each end of a basket of roses and small flowers, suspended by a ribbon bow. Trails of small flowers connect this part of the design to a circular garland of roses and a bow at each side The roses are padded and worked with straight stitches in silk ribbon in shades of pink. The small pale pink and blue flowers are worked in silk ribbon, either gathered into a circle or in straight stitches. The leaves are worked in green silk ribbon in small straight stitches. Stems are worked in stem stitch in olive green silk thread. The bow is in satin stitch in pale blue silk thread. The roses at the sides are formed with loops of shaded silk gauze ribbon, two loops to each of the five petals. The centres are worked in yellow silk thread in french knots. A cream silk cord, knotted at intervals, is sewn to the edge of the embroidered centre, with a frill of pale blue silk edged with pink shaded ribbon. The table centre is lined with silk.

Photograph Peter Henning

Teacosy
c. 1870 English
Designer and maker unknown
Beads and celluloid pearls on silk velvet
41 x 28 centimetres
Museum of Applied Arts and Sciences,
Sydney

An impressive accoutrement for the tea
table, this cosy is decorated with glass
beads in the style known as grisaille
work.

Photograph Penelope Clay

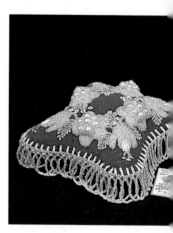

Pincushion
c. 1860 English or Australian
Designer and maker unknown
Beads and celluloid pearls on silk
velvet
16.5 x 18 centimetres
Historic Houses Trust of New South
Wales, Vaucluse House

Made to ornament a lady's dressing
table, pincushions like these were
used to store hatpins. They often
came with matching pockets for storing watches, which hung from the
dressing-table mirror posts.

Photograph Peter Henning

Apron
c. 1880 English
Designer and maker unknown
Steel beads on sateen (silk and cotton)
76 x 57 centimetres
Embroiderers Guild New South Wales,
Inc., Sydney

Impractical aprons like this were
decorative adjuncts to women's cos-
tume in the nineteenth century. They
were worn at afternoon tea when
friends came to call.

Photographs below Peter Henning
Photograph left David Liddle

Child's long robe
c. 1850 Australian
Attributed to Lady James Dowling (née Harriet Blaxland)
Cotton, broderie anglaise
53.5 x 85 centimetres
Historic Houses Trust of New South Wales, Vaucluse House, Sydney

The high-waisted, white cotton robe was sewn by hand. It incorporates insertions of Ayrshire embroidery and the sleeves are edged with broderie anglaise. Machine lace has also been used to detail the neckline. Stylistically, the garment dates from about 1850 and features a gauged and tucked waistline and horizontal hem tucks. It was handed down through the family for several generations and later entered the collection of Vaucluse House, Sydney.

Photographs Peter Henning

Carrickmacross lace fascinator
c. 1870 Australian
Designed and worked by Alice Cay
Cotton muslin on machine-made net
238 x 52 centimetres
North Shore Cavalcade of Fashion

This fascinator, or long head-scarf, has flowers appliquéd along its edges. It is finely worked and the array of flowers included is extensive. Alice Cay is said to have been inspired by the flowers from her own garden.

Photographs Peter Henning

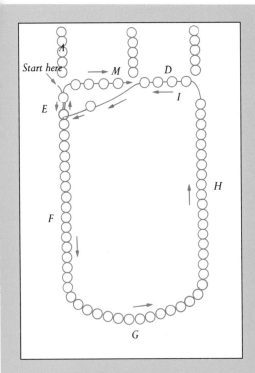

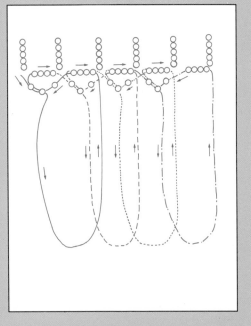

Schematic diagram of route for beading fringe

each bead. Stems from the large flowers are made of two strings of beads twisted together and couched down into place.

Sprays of five small white flowers are worked in the small white beads (600/11), using the backstitch method. Stitch nine beads around a small centre bead; the stems are crystal beads.

Once the beading of the main design is complete, carefully tear away the tissue paper. Leave the tacking rows around the edges of the velvet.

Fringe To make the fringe, you *must* wax the thread. To work the border, insert the threaded needle into the middle tacking line from the back of the fabric and bring it out to the right side. Thread on five opaque beads (A). Going in a straight line, insert the needle in the next tacking line (innermost one). Coming back up through where the thread was first inserted, thread four crystal beads on

the needle and take them along the middle tacking line (B). Take the thread underneath the fabric and insert it in the innermost tacking line; bring the thread out on the right side, thread on five opaque beads and bring the needle straight down to the crystal bead line, going along underneath the middle tacking line for the length of four beads (C). Come up to the right side and thread up with four crystal beads, and take the needle back to the base of the second string of opaque beads on the crystal bead line (D). Continue beading in this way right around these two lines of tacking around the pincushion until the first part of the fringe is complete on all sides. With a separate thread couch down between each bead.

To make the looped edge of the fringe, work from left to right. Thread up with waxed thread and, working along the crystal bead line of the row just worked (the middle row of tacking), bring the needle out of the fabric at the

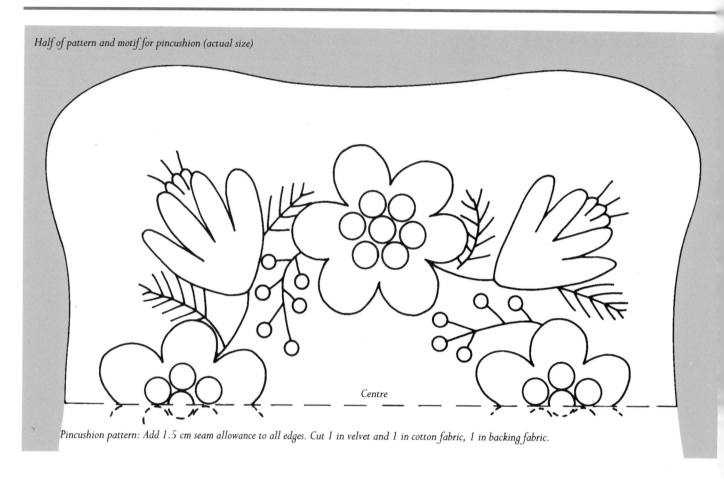

Half of pattern and motif for pincushion (actual size)

Centre

Pincushion pattern: Add 1.5 cm seam allowance to all edges. Cut 1 in velvet and 1 in cotton fabric, 1 in backing fabric.

base of the opaque beads. Thread one crystal bead on, then one opaque bead (E), then seventeen crystal beads (F), followed by fifteen opaque beads (G), followed by eighteen crystal beads (H). Miss one opaque bead line (vertical line) and insert the needle through next four crystal beads (I). Come back to the base of the missed opaque bead line, and bring the needle out (J). Thread one crystal bead (K) on and then thread through the first opaque bead at the start of the loop (L), then thread back through the first bead on the loop, then across through four crystal beads on the beaded border (M). Continue in this way, crossing over the loops of fringe until the work is completed.

Finishing

Remove the two inner tacking threads. Make sure that the fringe is not caught in the seam line (outermost row of tacking), then pin the backing fabric in place; right sides together, leaving an opening for pushing the stuffing through. Tack the pieces together, then machine around the tacking line. Trim back the seam allowance. Turn the cushion right side out, and fill it with washed lambswool or polyfill or scraps of woollen yarn. Turn in the seam allowance at the opening and slipstitch or topstitch together to close.

* The beads and pearls, and other beading supplies, may be obtained by mail order from Photios Bros (66 Druitt Street, Sydney, 2000) by quoting the numbers listed. *Start here*

June Powys

BEADED VELVET TEACOSY

Finished size

29 x 42 centimetres

Materials

- ❖ 70 centimetres of 115 centimetre wide blue velvet
- ❖ 40 centimetres of 115 millimetre wide lawn to back the velvet
- ❖ 80 centimetres of coarse string covered with a bias strip of the velvet
- ❖ Ten 8 millimetre pearl beads
- ❖ Rocaille beads, 2 millimetres*
    546 or 411 silver steel
    281 clear crystal
    309 opaque or milk bead
    311/8 white
- ❖ No. 14 beading needle
- ❖ Gütermann Polytwist: white thread for beading, blue thread for making up
- ❖ Round-ended bodkin
- ❖ 1 teacosy pad
- ❖ Tissue or tracing paper

Method

Both sides of the beaded teacosy are the same measurements. Cut two pieces of velvet measuring 32 x 45 centimetres, and two pieces of lawn to the same measurement. Tack the lawn to the back of the velvet pieces. Cut 4 centimetre wide bias strips if necessary to cover the string to make a rouleau trim (instructions below).

Outline the shape of the cosy on the two pieces of velvet with a tacking stitch. Mark vertical and horizontal centre lines in tacking on the cosy. Enlarge the pattern using the enlarger on a photocopier or by scaling up using the grid provided (see chapter 6). Trace the design onto tissue paper and, matching the centre lines on the velvet and the pattern, tack the tissue paper onto the fabric, and work the beading through

Such elaborate tea-time accessories were much loved in the Victorian era, and here we describe how to re-create one of these treasured beauties.

the paper. It would be best to work the design with the fabric in a frame.

Beading Read the general notes on beading on page 25. Start with the central motif, the large flower. (This flower is, however, slightly off-centre.) Attach the large centre pearl first. Make separate strings of the white and clear beads and twist them around each other. Fill in the flower petals with these twisted strings, working first in a circular movement around the centre of flower, and couching the twists down. Then fill in the petal shapes with the same twists, couching the twists down onto the tissue paper. Using the method of attaching individual beads with a backstitch, sew a row of clear beads around the outline of the petals.

The thistle-like bud shapes at the centre should be worked next. The top of the bud is padded, so use the trapunto quilting method described for the Vaucluse House pincushion for padding these before commencing beading. Work the base of the bud first by attaching a large pearl bead and then using twists of beads for the petals in the same way as for the centre of the large flower. Bead the centre of the bud with silver beads (these were steel in original cosy). Next fill in the rest of the bud on either side using the backstitch method with individual beads. They could also be filled in with small strings of beads of appropriate size to fit the design. In this method, attach the thread at one end of the upper part of the bud, thread beads on until there are enough to fill that particular line, and take the thread down at the other end of the design line. Couch down between each bead with a separate thread.

To complete the centre of the design, make the twisted stem from the large flower with a

Teacosy
c. 1870 English
Designer and maker unknown
Beads and celluloid pearls on silk velvet
41 x 28 centimetres
Museum of Applied Arts and Sciences, Sydney

An impressive accoutrement for the tea table, this cosy is decorated with glass beads in the style known as grisaille work.

Photograph Penelope Clay
Illustrated in colour on page 28

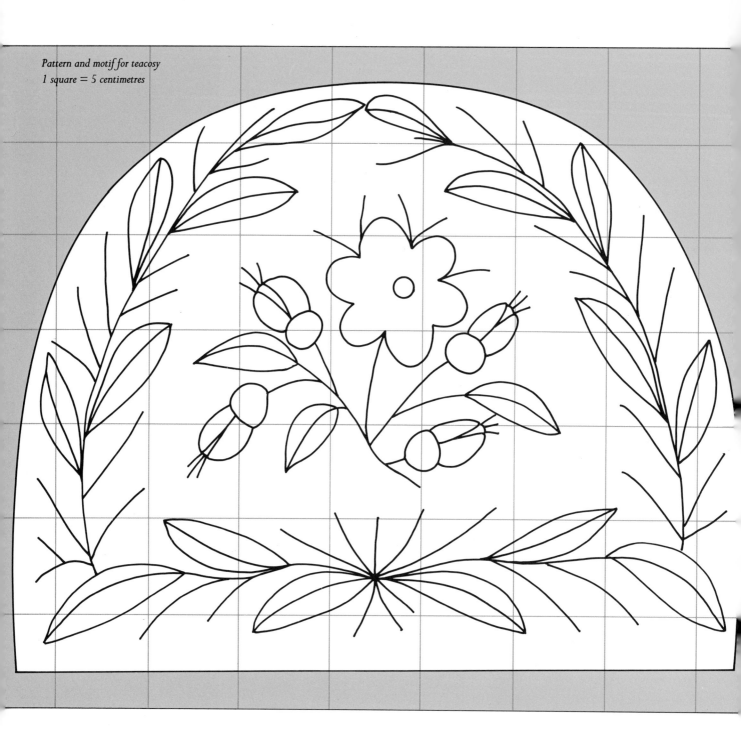

Pattern and motif for teacosy
1 square = 5 centimetres

string of white and string of clear glass beads, of the appropriate length, twisted together and couched down into place. Repeat this method for shorter twisted stems from buds.

Couch down the other stems in clear glass beads, then, making small strings of beads to the correct size of the leaf, couch down between each bead with a separate thread.

The leaves and sprays and stems on the outer edge can be worked in the short strings of beads method, with couching down between each bead. The large leaves have opaque or milk beads on one side and white beads on the other half.

When one side of the tea cosy is completed, work the second in the same way.

Finishing

Once the beading is complete, carefully tear away the tissue paper. The shape for the cosy can now be cut out, leaving a 1.5 centimetre seam allowance on all sides.

Matching the centres at the top, tack the two sides together down from the centre. Machine together. Turn right side out. Make two separate strings of white and glass beads long enough, when twisted together, to go over the whole length of the curved edge and attach by couching to cover the seam line.

Make up 40 centimetres of bias rouleau-covered string with the bias strip of velvet for the bow on top of the cosy. To make corded rouleau, the amount of cord required is twice that of the finished rouleau length. Fold the fabric in half along its length, right sides together. Using the machine zipper foot, stitch through the bias and the cord at the midpoint of the cord, bringing the stitching beyond the cord. This allows for ease when turning the fabric. Then stitch along the length of the bias close to the cord. Grasp the end of the cord at the covered end and turn the fabric through to the right side by carefully easing it over the

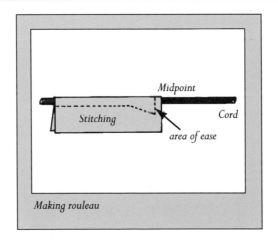

Making rouleau

uncovered end to make the covered cord. Attach this to the cosy and then attach a twisted string of white and glass beads to the three loops of the bow. Each loop of the bow is 10 centimetres long, so cut 10 centimetre lengths and finish the edges by pushing the fabric in over the string and top sewing the ends. Attach the loops at the top of the cosy after bending them into a bow shape.

Insert the tea cosy pad and turn in the seam allowance along the base of the teacosy and slipstitch it to the base of the pad. Then make two separate strings of white and clear glass beads long enough so that, when twisted together, they will fit around the base of the cosy. Attach the bead twist by couching it in place.

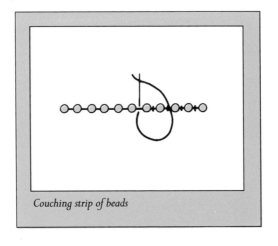

Couching strip of beads

* The beads and pearls, and other beading supplies, may be obtained by mail order from Photios Bros (66 Druitt Street, Sydney, 2000) by quoting the numbers listed.

VICTORIAN BEADED APRON

June Powy

A beaded satin apron is an unlikely dress accessory today, but the floral motifs on this piece are lovely. The design from the bib could be used on a black satin bag for evening wear (for which we give instructions), beaded in silver steel seed beads. The motif and the border design, which we also include, could also be used on clothing.

Detail of apron
c. 1880 English
Designer and maker unknown
Steel beads on sateen (silk and cotton)
76 x 57 centimetres
Embroiderers Guild New South
Wales, Inc., Sydney

Impractical aprons like this were decorative adjuncts to women's costume in the nineteenth century. They were worn at afternoon tea when friends came to call.

Photograph Peter Henning

* These beads may be obtained by mail order from Photios Bros (66 Druitt Street, Sydney, 2000) by quoting the numbers listed.

Finished size

A clutch bag 18 x 15 centimetres.

Materials

❖ 40 x 25 centimetre piece of black satin for bag
❖ 40 x 25 centimetre piece of black lining fabric
❖ 40 x 25 centimetre piece of interfacing (choose its weight to suit the firmness you want in the finished bag)
❖ Rocaille silver steel beads 546 or 411*
❖ Gütermann Polytwist black thread
❖ No. 14 beading needle
❖ Tissue paper

Method

To make a clutch bag, first mark tacking lines on the piece of satin to mark for the flap and where the fold for the base of bag is to be.

Transfer the embroidery design from the pattern onto tissue paper and tack this into place on the right side of the flap. Use a frame and bead by picking up individual beads and backstitching them into place, working on top of the design, through the tissue paper and fabric (see the general directions on beading on page 25). When the beading is completed, carefully tear the tissue paper away.

Cut out the lining for the bag.

Finishing

Join up the side seams of the bag, and then of the lining, taking up a slightly larger seam allowance for the lining than the bag. With the bag turned right side out and the wrong side of the lining to the outside, insert the lining into the bag and slipstitch the lining across the bag opening and around the edges of the flap. Place invisible press studs inside the flap. Press carefully with a steam iron if necessary to complete the bag, but take care to avoid the beading.

Using the designs

The design on the bib of the apron could also be used on the shoulder of a black crêpe frock. The large design on the front of apron could be divided into two halves and used on the fronts of a black woollen cardigan and worked in silver steel beads or shiny black beads. Use a backing fabric of organza (see the general directions on beading on page 25), and use the tissue method for transferring the design onto the cardigan. The design on the front of the apron could be used on the yoke of a black crêpe frock, or down the centre of the sleeves of a frock, using half the design on each sleeve, or on the front of a blouse. Work the beading before making up sleeves. This beading would be done using the tissue paper and backstitch method.

Motifs from apron (actual size)

Border pattern

Bib pattern

Whitework

*I*t has often been claimed that whitework—embroidery worked with a white thread on a white ground—is the best way to show one's talent in needlework. This is because the stitches must always maintain a smooth, even quality so that they will blend perfectly with the background.

Whitework may be divided into two basic types: 'open', in which the pattern is produced by the arrangement of the holes cut and overcast, and 'close', in which the stitches are worked upon the foundation, like surface embroidery. The term also has wider application and covers various types of pulled fabric and drawn thread work as well as plain sewing.

Another important characteristic is that whitework has been used traditionally for articles that require frequent washing: collars, cuffs, engageantes (undersleeves), aprons, undergarments, children's clothing, household linen, tablecloths and ecclesiastical vestments are some of the many examples that spring to mind.

By the late eighteenth century, whitework in Europe was used almost exclusively with costume. The growing demand for lighter fabrics and simpler styles of dress lead to the establishment of a number of whitework industries. Some operated solely on a cottage basis. Others, like Dresden work, were highly commercialised and supplied a wide domestic and export market. This luxurious trade embroidery resembled the effect of bobbin lace. It was used mainly for ruffles on men's and women's clothing.

Whitework embroidery received another boost after the French Revolution, when women of fashion began to wear simple, classically inspired dresses. These garments had a delicate, almost transparent appearance and were decorated very simply with white sprigs and borders worked in tambouring. Initially, such dresses were made from imported Indian muslin, but by the early nineteenth century, muslin factories had been established in Scotland and elsewhere to meet local demand. Whitework embroidery on women's dresses was briefly revived again during the 1830s.

Advances in weaving techniques, together with the ready availability of cotton from the southern states of America, led to the increased production of fabrics throughout the British Isles generally. Moreover, the mechanisation of textile production in Scotland coincided with the development of a large horizontal embroidery frame, which allowed several embroiderers to work simultaneously on one piece.

In 1782 an Italian, Luigi Ruffini, set up a workroom in Edinburgh for the production of 'flowered' or embroidered muslin. The sewed-muslin industry soon became highly organised, with similar workshops being established in other Scottish cities such as Glasgow and Paisley. Agents were appointed to supervise the embroiderers, who worked in their own homes. Women and older girls produced the floral motifs with a tambour hook, which formed a continuous chain stitch.

Another important trade embroidery, Ayrshire work, takes its name from the county in south-west Scotland where the technique originated. It was also produced on the Scottish west coast and in Ireland. Ayrshire work dates back to 1814, when a sewed-muslin agent, Mrs Jamieson of Ayr, began copying some of the pulled work stitches (known as 'French lace') worked on a christening robe recently brought back from France. These stitches were taught to some of her employees, and the technique quickly spread, supplanting the earlier tambour work.

Traditionally, Ayrshire embroidery was worked in fine cotton thread on a muslin ground. It combined padded satin stitch and stem stitch with drawn thread work and fine needlepoint infilling to achieve a lace-like effect, using predominantly floral motifs. Most Ayrshire work took the form of insertions and appeared on christening robes, ladies' dresses,

The Vaucluse House doll Charlotte is illustrated
on page 55. Here are the two pieces from her
wardrobe for which we give patterns, the apron
(above) and chemise (right).

Historic Houses Trust of New South Wales,
Vaucluse House, Sydney
Photograph Peter Henning

Below: Kangaroo Apple Kangaroo Needlerun lace fan
c. 1910 Tasmanian
Designed by Miss M.E. (Patty) Mault and worked by Miss
A.G. Wilson
Width 38 centimetres
Tasmanian Museum and Art Gallery, Hobart
No pattern

Detail of an adaptation of
Purple creeper and wild weed
lace
c. 1910, 1989.
Original design by Miss M.
Hope (see page 57), adapted
by Marie Laurie
Cotton and linen
Width of lace 5 centimetres
Maker's collection

The lacemaker here has
adapted Miss Hope's design
to make a corner and edge for
a modern-sized handkerchief.

Photograph David Liddle

Jug cover
c. 1930 Probably Australian
Designer and maker unknown
Cream cotton with blue plastic beads
Diameter 234 millimetres
Museum of Applied Arts and Sciences, Sydney

The central feature of this round cotton jug cover is a closely
worked three-dimensional cup and saucer. From this motif, an
eighteen-point star design radiates out into an open mesh
ground. The border is edged with three rows of crocheted scal-
lops and is decorated with thirty-five blue beads, which also act
as weights, keeping the cover in place while in use.

Large numbers of crochet and crochet-trimmed food covers
have been made in Australia to keep the ever-present flies at
bay. The teacup was a common decorative motif on milk jug
covers in the 1930s, and highlights the importance of teatime
in people's lives. Three-dimensional work became more common
during the crochet vogue of the early 1900s and the surviving
examples of mirror covers, bowls, hats and other items reflect an
effort to find new applications for the crochet technique.

Photograph Penelope Clay

...awls and petticoats, as well as collars, cuffs ...nd men's shirt frills.

This technique was admired enormously for ...s incredible fineness and delicacy. However, ...he close, detailed work also caused severe eye-...rain and, according to contemporary reports, ...any women bathed their eyes with whisky to ...btain some relief. Ayrshire work went into ...ecline during the American Civil War, when ...he trade in cotton was interrupted. Machine ...mbroidery had also become feasible by this ...ime and its possibilities were soon recognised ...y manufacturers. Yet another reason was the ...evelopment in England during the 1840s of a ...nore simplified form of decorative whitework ...nown as broderie anglaise.

Although coarser in appearance, broderie ...nglaise was still effective and had the advantage ...f being executed more easily. It consisted of ...noles cut into muslin, cotton or linen and ...mbellished with buttonhole or a close overcast ...stitch. These holes were round, oval or leaf-...shaped. Most of the designs were based on con-...ventional, repeating patterns and left little ...scope for creativity. Broderie anglaise remained ...popular until well into the twentieth century, ...although machinery had largely taken over from ...handwork by this time. It was used for under-...garments, particularly petticoats, and children's ...clothing.

Countless christening robes and babies' dress-es have survived from the colonial period in Australia because of their heirloom value. In most cases, however, nothing is known about their makers, their date and place of execution, or the circumstances under which they were originally produced. One exception is the child's long robe illustrated on page 30, which has been attributed to Harriet Dowling, née Blaxland. Harriet herself belonged to an important colonial family, being the daughter of John Blaxland, and she would have received early instruction in both plain sewing and embroidery. She also made two

judicious marriages. After the death of her first husband, Arthur Macdonald Ritchie, she married Sir James Dowling, who served as chief justice of New South Wales between 1837 and 1844. Harriet became stepmother to Dowling's six children and lived with her family at Brougham Lodge in the Sydney suburb of Woolloomooloo.

Throughout the colonial period, needlework formed an important part of a young girl's edu-cation and training commenced from early childhood.

The making of dolls' clothes was seen as another important part of this educational process. Flora Glickmann wrote at length on the subject in her book *The Cult of the Needle* (London, 1915) and claimed that it provided invaluable training for marriage and motherhood.

The little girl who had taken a part in making her doll's wardrobe, and then in keeping it up-to-date, will find that the knowledge she has gained in this way will be invaluable to her in after life. The child who has helped to put together her doll's combinations, will have no difficul-ty in making her own later on, neither will she be per-plexed when she in turn has little people to sew for.

The doll from Vaucluse House, Charlotte, illustrated on page 55, was named after her original owner, Charlotte Davies, and has been handed down through the family from mother to daughter. She was manufactured in England about 1870. While her first set of clothes was probably sewn commercially and sold with the doll, these were supplemented later by hand-made garments. Together they form a docu-ment of the types of clothing worn by children during the nineteenth century.

Charlotte's dress is made of cream tussore silk. It dates stylistically from about 1865–70 and has two rows of very tight pleats on the skirt, bodice and sleeves. Charlotte also has a fringed shawl made of silk. Only some of the other garments in the doll's extensive wardrobe of dresses including a petticoat, drawers, under-bodice, chemise and apron are illustrated here.

AN INFANT'S LONG ROBE

Lindie War

*T*his long robe from Vaucluse House has a wealth of fine detail. Such a long robe for a baby would make a suitable christening gown today.

Clothing Patterns

In the following patterns, we have given you as much information as will enable you to reproduce these garments. By all means cut down the time they take by using the sewing machine, especially where it doesn't show, but the instructions tell you how the pieces were made originally.

The instructions are not intended for anyone who has not sewn before, although the doll's underwear is simple enough for someone who hasn't done much sewing. The long robe more complicated and also requires very fine workmanship.

Actual size patterns have been included; this minimises error. Label each pattern piece as it is made and mark on grain lines and any other essential marks, such as centre front.

Where the pattern pieces are squares and rectangles, cut on the grain of the fabric; this is easier and more accurate, and the garment will sit better.

When I refer to the left and right sides of a garment, it is as if it is being worn.

Finished size

Length 103 centimetres

Materials

❖ 1.8 metres of 115 centimetre wide very fine white cotton lawn
❖ 30 centimetres of 115 centimetre wide fine white muslin for yoke, neck and waist binding
❖ 1.2 metres of embroidered muslin (very fine broderie anglaise) with a Van Dyke edge, 3 millimetres wide
❖ 20 centimetres of embroidered muslin (very fine broderie anglaise) insertion, 18 millimetres wide
❖ 50 centimetres of fine cord, 1 millimetre wide, for the front smocking
❖ 1.1 metres of cotton lace, 12 millimetre wide, for the neck and yoke
❖ 2 metres of cotton tape, 4 millimetres wide for the yoke, neck and waist
❖ 60 centimetres of piping cord, 2 millimetres wide
❖ White polyester sewing machine thread
❖ White DMC broder machine cotton no. 50 (very fine thread)
❖ DMC stranded cotton in white
❖ 1 mother-of-pearl button, 7 millimetre diameter

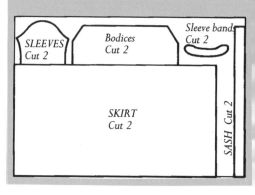

Pattern layout for lawn

SLEEVES Cut 2

Bodices Cut 2

Sleeve bands Cut 2

SKIRT Cut 2

SASH Cut 2

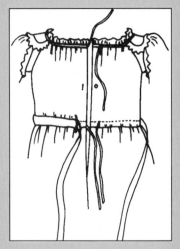

Detail of back

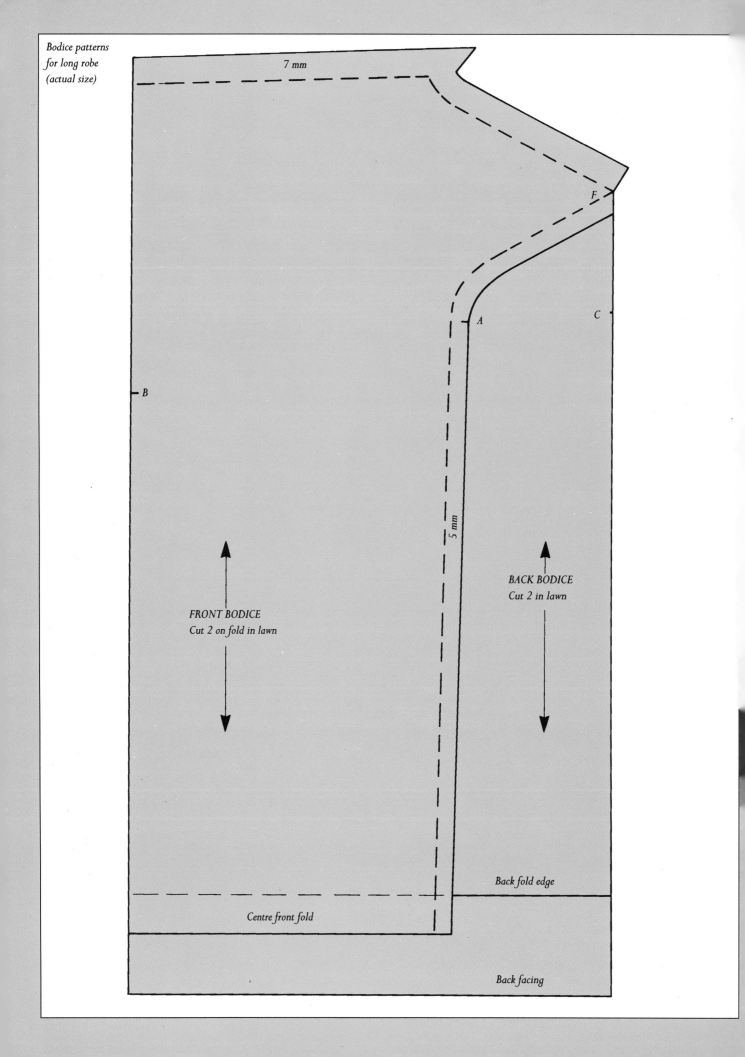

Bodice patterns
for long robe
(actual size)

7 mm

F

C

A

B

5 mm

FRONT BODICE
Cut 2 on fold in lawn

BACK BODICE
Cut 2 in lawn

Back fold edge

Centre front fold

7 mm

Back facing

Patterns for sleeve and sleeveband (actual size)

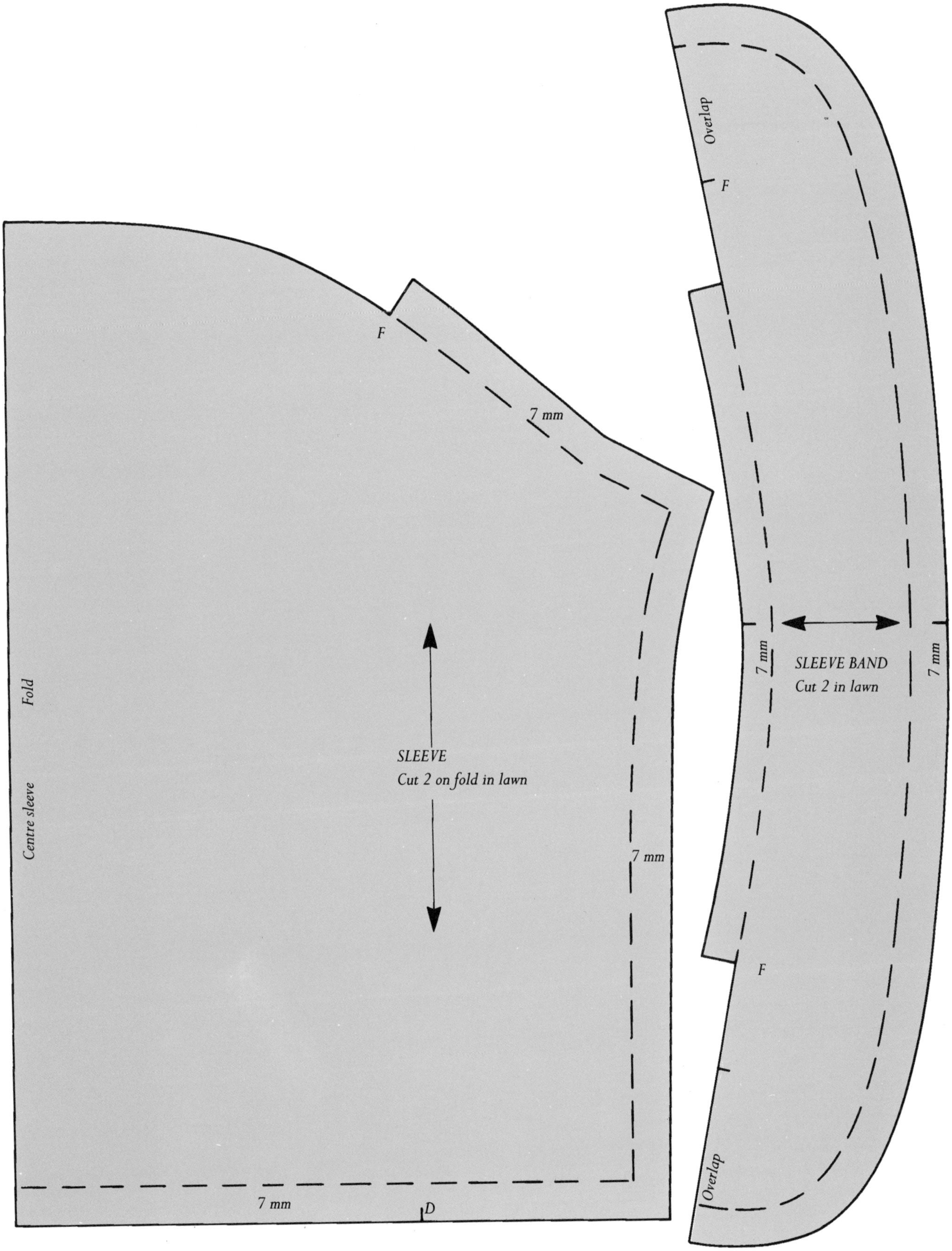

Overlap

F

7 mm

F

Fold

Centre sleeve

SLEEVE
Cut 2 on fold in lawn

7 mm

7 mm

7 mm

SLEEVE BAND
Cut 2 in lawn

7 mm

F

7 mm

D

Overlap

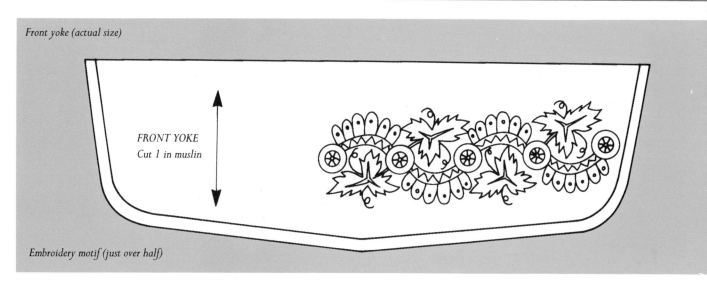

Front yoke (actual size)

FRONT YOKE
Cut 1 in muslin

Embroidery motif (just over half)

Method

The pattern consists of front and back bodice, sleeve, sleeveband and yoke (actual-size patterns). Cut the yoke in muslin but the rest of the pieces in lawn. For the skirt, cut two rectangles 102 centimetres wide and 57 centimetres long; for the sash, cut two 72 centimetre lengths, 7 centimetres wide with a selvage down one side, in lawn. In muslin, cut straight-grain strips 18 millimetres wide and totalling 1 metre in length; and two bias strips 16 millimetres wide, each 25 centimetres long.

A seam allowance of 7 millimetres has been included throughout, except where the yoke meets the bodice, where 5 millimetres has been allowed.

The original long robe had extremely fine french seams that finished 2 millimetres wide. I have allowed 7 millimetres for the french seams but if you are prefer to make them finer you can trim this down.

If you have the time, work a row of drawn thread work on each edge of the embroidered insertion on the cuff.

Mark the centres of the front, skirt, sleeve

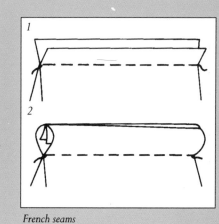

French seams

Roll and whip hem

Roll and whip and attach lace

It is also possible to roll and whip and gather and attach lace in one process, if you prefer.

nd yoke pieces with contrasting thread before ou gather them.

oke and front bodice Embroider the muslin yoke. Draw up the embroidery design to he full yoke width and transfer it to the yoke by racing. Use a very sharp pencil (an F grade pencil is best) or water-erasable pen. If you use the pen, wash the piece very thoroughly in cold water when you have finished the embroidery.

Cut 35 centimetres of lace edging and gather t up to measure 21 centimetres.

Roll the sides and bottom edge of the yoke under 3 millimetres and whip the gathered lace to the yoke.

Before gathering the top edge of the front bodice, mark for gathering on its lower edge dots 1 centimetre apart from B to B, in three rows, starting 7 millimetres in from the edge, then 10 millimetres, then 1 centimetre. Sew the three rows of gathering stitches for smocking but don't draw them up yet.

Now work two rows of gathering from A to A across the front neck of the front bodice, with the second row 5 millimetres from the top edge. Use a very small, neat running stitch to do this. Draw up the gathers. Pin the yoke in place on top of the front bodice, arranging the gathers carefully so they are even. (You could now draw up the gathers on the lower edge of the bodice to 8 centimetres to help make the gathers even.)

Work a running stitch around the edge of the yoke, securing it to the bodice. Trim the raw edges on the inside to a minimum.

Cut 25 centimetres of 4 millimetre tape and hem it to the inside edge of the yoke to cover the raw edges; mitre the corners.

Smocking Gather up the lower front to measure 8 centimetres (if you haven't already done so) and tie off.

Cut four pieces of cord each 96 millimetres long. Lay the cord along the top row of gathering and couch it into place with a fine thread. Leave the ends raw because they will be covered by the belt. Couch the other three pieces of cord into place as shown in the diagram. Embroider the two horizontal lines of satin stitch dots with two strands of white stranded cotton and two stitches per dot.

Back bodice Fold the fabric at centre back 27 millimetres under, then turn the edge in 7 millimetres and hem on the inside. Work this hem on each side. On one back piece, make two rows of gathering (in a small, fine running stitch) along the neck from C to the centre back, and pull in to measure 9.5 centimetres and fasten off the gathering. Repeat on the other side.

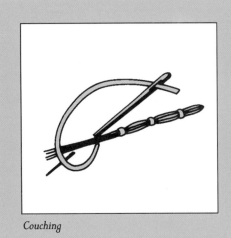

Couching

Detail of smocking, centre front
Embroidered dots   *Fine cord*

— 2 mm
— 4 mm
— 2 mm
— 4 mm
— 4 mm

Note that, for clarity, the satin stitch dots are shown larger than you would work them.

Smocking

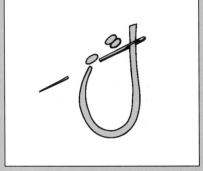

Satin stitch dots

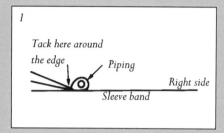

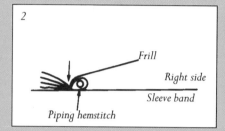

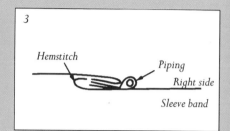

Sleeve band edging

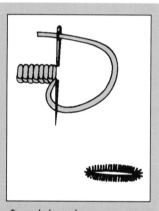

Buttonhole stitch

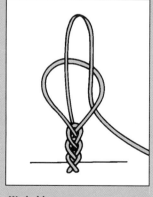

Worked loop

Join the front and back bodice side seams together with french seams.

Sleeves Fold a 30 centimetre piece of bias muslin in half and lay 30 centimetres of piping cord in the fold. Sew close to the cord with a running stitch (use a zipper foot if you are sewing by machine). With a sleeve shoulder band right side up, lay the piping around the curved outside edge, and tack it into place 7 millimetres in from the edge.

Cut 48 centimetres of embroidered edging and gather to 28.5 centimetres. Place this right side down on top of the piping, with the edges together, and sew through the three layers, allowing extra gathering on the corners to avoid flattening the lace here. The frill, the piping and the sleeveband are now joined. Trim away the excess edges of the frill and piping, leaving the edge of the sleeve shoulder band to cover the raw edges. Turn this edge under 3 millimetres and hem along the underside of the frill.

On the sleeve, work two rows of gathering at the head from F to F and at the cuff from D to D; the second row of stitching should be 7 millimetres from the edge. Use a small neat running stitch. Gather in the cuff to measure 7.5 centimetres from edge to edge. Secure the ends.

Cuff With right sides together, sew 7.5 centimetres of insertion to the lower sleeve. Trim the edge of the insertion to 3 millimetres and turn the sleeve edge over it like a run and fell seam, but only tack it at present, because you will now work two rows of staggered double satin stitch

dots around the top of the insertion to hold the seam down.

Now join a 7.5 millimetre piece of embroidered edging (not gathered) to the insertion in the same way. The cuff is now complete.

Now make a french seam in the sleeve.

Place the centre of the finished sleeve shoulder band on the bodice side seam, right sides together. Sew it in place up to the top of the bodice armhole, taking care not to catch the lace into the stitching. Pin the sleeve band to overlap front over back, measuring 6.5 centimetres from the front sleeve seam to the back sleeve seam.

Gather in the sleeve head. Place the sleeve on top of the sleeve band, pin them together, and adjust the gathers at the sleeve head. Sew the sleeve and bodice together with a small running stitch, strengthening it with a backstitch every few stitches. Neaten the seam by trimming the edges of the sleeve and the bodice to 3 centimetres and folding the sleeveband edge over and hemming it down.

Neck edge Gathered up, the neck should measure, from centre back edge to armhole, 9.5 centimetres; across the top of the armhole, 6.5 centimetres; and across the top of the front yoke, 15 centimetres. The total length edge to edge is 48 centimetres.

On a 50 centimetre piece of straight muslin, fold the edge in 1 centimetre and place it on the left back edge. With right sides together and raw edges melting, sew it along the neckline, 5 millimetres in from the edge, with a small running stitch.

Work a buttonhole 4 millimetres wide and 2 centimetres in from the centre back edge on the right side.

For the back tie, cut 77 centimetres of 4 millimetre cotton tape. Fold the binding over the edge to finish 5 millimetres wide and hem, inserting the tape into the binding as you go so it enters into the left back edge and exits through the buttonhole on the right.

For the neck edge, finish the ends of a 72 centimetre piece of lace edging with a fine hem, and gather it into 48 centimetres. Whip this lace around the top of the neck binding.

Lower bodice edge Sew two rows of gathering from B to the back edge of the back bodice. Pull the fabric in to measure 13 centimetres from the side seam to the back edge.

The front bodice should measure 24 centimetres, and the complete lower edge, 50 centimetres.

Place a length of straight-grain muslin, 52 centimetres long and 18 millimetres wide, on the left bodice edge and work around the whole bodice in the same way as the neck edge, inserting 77 centimetres of 4 millimetre tape into the binding and making a buttonhole on the right side. Work a double row of satin stitch dots along the binding just at the bottom of the front smocking.

Skirt Fold the widest side of one of the skirt pieces in half and cut an opening along the fold 19 centimetres long for the back opening. Make a tiny rolled hem on the left side.

Fold the left side back 1.5 centimetres, turn in the edge and hem. Measure 6 millimetres to the right of the bottom of the opening and mark the point (X on the diagram). Move the left side over to the X. Stitch across the bottom of the placket securely with a backstitch.

Now join the front and back of the skirt, with french seams at the sides, and press.

The tucked hem Fold the hem up 5 centimetres, turn the edge under 5 millimetres, press and hem on the inside.

Waistline Fold the top of the skirt down 1 centimetres. Mark the top as for smocking, with dots 1 centimetres apart and 2 millimetres and 6 millimetres down from the folded edge. Work running stitch, and pull in the gathering threads to measure 48 centimetres and secure the ends. Distribute the gathers evenly.

Securely stitch the edge of the folds to the edge of the waistband.

Sash Make a fine rolled hem on the long raw edges of the two sash lengths. Turn a 1 centimetre hem at one end of each sash; sew a running stitch through the other end and pull it in to measure 2 centimetres.

Place this gathered end of the sash across the front smocking right sides together, and stitch it to the edge of the smocking panel. Fold sash over and topstitch it down. Repeat on other side.

Make a worked loop 2 centimetres in from the left back and 2 centimetres long, to hold the sash in the waistline.

Work a buttonhole on the left side 8 millimetres long midway between the neck and waist. Finally attach a corresponding button to the right side.

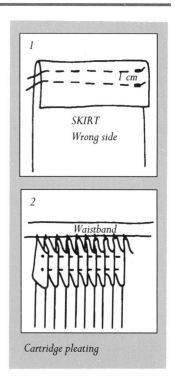

Cartridge pleating

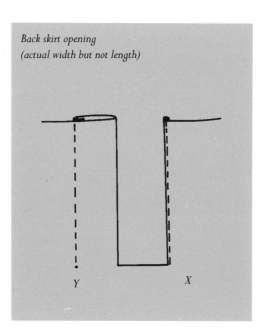

Back skirt opening (actual width but not length)

DOLL'S CLOTHING FOR CHARLOTTE

Lindie Ward

*C*harlotte's owner provided her with a full wardrobe of clothing. Here we give patterns for her chemise and apron.

Charlotte's measurements are:
Chest   26 centimetres
Across chest to shoulders   12 centimetres
Head to toe   48.5 centimetres
Neck to waist   10.5 centimetres
Skirt length   27 centimetres
Waist to toe   30.5 centimetres

CHEMISE

Finished size

Length 27.5 centimetres

Materials

❖ 30 centimetres of 90 centimetre wide fine white lawn
❖ White machine sewing thread
❖ 40 centimetres of white insertion lace 18 millimetres wide
❖ 1.6 metres of lace edging 15 millimetres wide
❖ 1 mother-of-pearl button 5 millimetres in diameter

Method

The pattern consists of the front and back chemise and sleeve (actual size patterns). A 5 millimetre seam allowance is included throughout for side seams and sleeves, and a 3 millimetre allowance for the rolled edges.

Cut a 4.5 centimetre long opening at the centre front of the front chemise.

Work run and fell seams on the sleeves and side seams.

Chemise for Charlotte

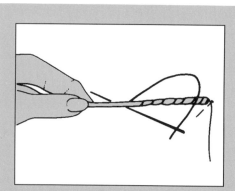

Roll and whip hem

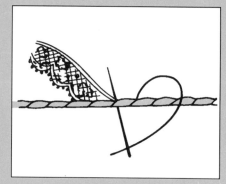

Roll and whip and attach lace
It is also possible to roll and whip and gather and attach lace lace in one process, if you prefer.

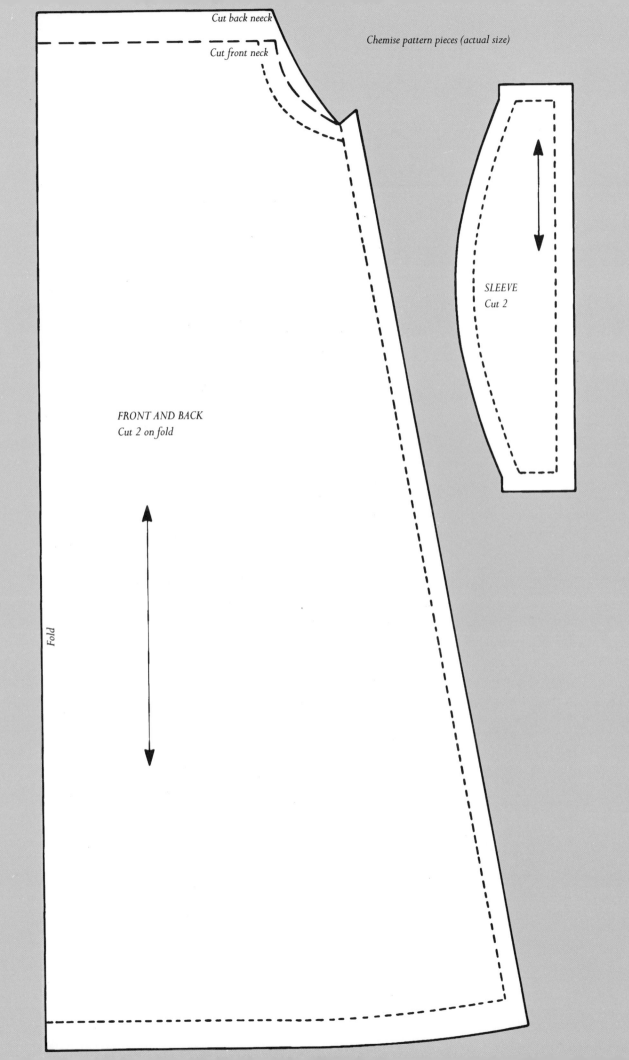

Cut back neeck

Cut front neck

Chemise pattern pieces (actual size)

SLEEVE
Cut 2

FRONT AND BACK
Cut 2 on fold

Fold

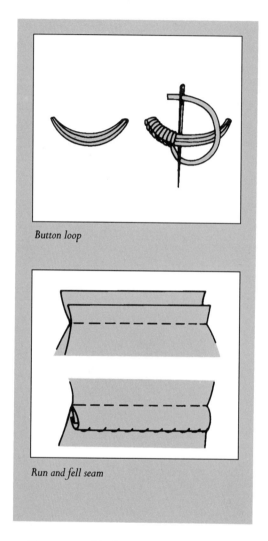

Button loop

Run and fell seam

by whipping the edge, using a running stitch, or by drawing up a thread at the edge of the lace. Pin the lace in place on each side of the lace insertion and sew a mitred corner at the bottom of the centre front opening. Starting on the left front, roll the neck edge and simultaneously whip the insertion lace and gathered lace edging together Then continue back around again, whipping the gathered lace to the insertion to finish back on the left side.

Make two circular bands of edging lace one and a half times width of the sleeve and whip each one to the rolled sleeve edge.

Finishing

Make a fine rolled hem on the left side of the front opening through the lace edge, insertion and chemise front, and stitch the bottom of the centre front opening securely.

Finish the bottom of the chemise with a fine double hem.

Finally, sew the button to the left side where the insertion joins the chemise and work a corresponding loop on the right side, on the edge of the insertion.

APRON

Finished size

Top of apron bodice 12 centimetres wide, 23.5 centimetres long

Materials

❖ 25 centimetres of 90 centimetre wide fine white muslin
❖ 3.5 metres of edging lace 1.5 centimetres wide
❖ 70 centimetres of insertion lace 2 centimetres wide
❖ White machine sewing thread

Sleeves Fold the 5 millimetre armhole seam back and whip the sleeves and the body together. Finish each side of the seam with a double fold and hemming stitch.

The top of the sleeve should measure 3.5 centimetres from seam to seam across the shoulder.

Lace Pin the lace insertion to the right front opening and around the now square neckline, mitring the corners at the centre front and each of the four sleeve seams.

Cut a length of lace edging twice the length of the neckline and front opening, plus another length to gather in. Gather the lace

❖ 75 centimetres of apricot silk ribbon 2.5 centimetres wide

❖ Loop and rouleau turner

Method

The pattern pieces for the apron are cut as strips of fabric:

for the upper skirt, cut a rectangle 16 x 39 centimetres,

for the lower skirt, cut a rectangle 14 x 39 centimetres,

for the bodice, cut a rectangle 19.5 x 4.5 centimetres,

for the waistband, cut a rectangle 21 x 2.8 centimetres, and

for the straps cut two strips 15 x 2 centimetres. Cut all of these pieces on the straight grain of the fabric.

A seam allowance of 5 millimetres has been included throughout. The seams on this apron are finely rolled, then the two edges are whipped together.

Bodice Fold the top and bottom edges of the bodice (the longest edges) over 5 millimetres and press. Run a gathering stitch along these edges. Use a small, neat running stitch. Gather the top into 9 centimetres and the bottom into 8 centimetres in width.

With the two muslin straps (15 centimetre long strips) make two rouleaux 5 millimetres wide: fold the strips in half lengthwise; stitch 5 millimetres from the fold (use a very small machine stitch); trim the seam allowance; turn right side out using a loop turner. Attach the straps to each corner of the top bodice, 5 millimetres in from the edge.

Cut 25 centimetres of lace and gather it with running stitch, or by whipping, or by drawing up a thread in the edge, but leave the last 4 centimetres ungathered. The whole piece should measure 18 centimetres when gathered. Roll the side edge of the bodice under and

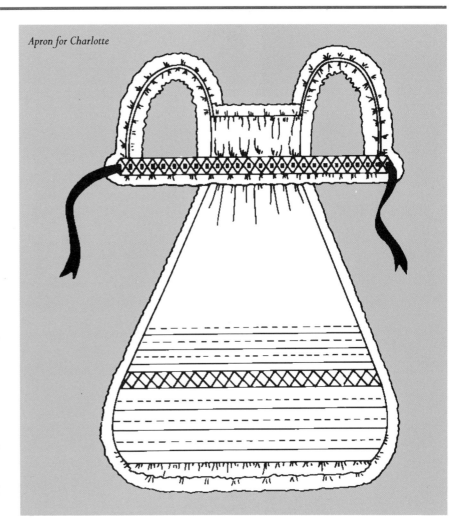

Apron for Charlotte

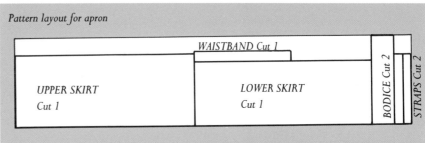

Pattern layout for apron

simultaneously whip the ungathered part of the lace to it and the gathered part all around inside of the strap. Repeat on the other side.

Press a 5 millimetre hem all around the edge of the 21 centimetre muslin waistband. Pin and tack the insertion lace on top of the muslin

Template for apron skirt hem

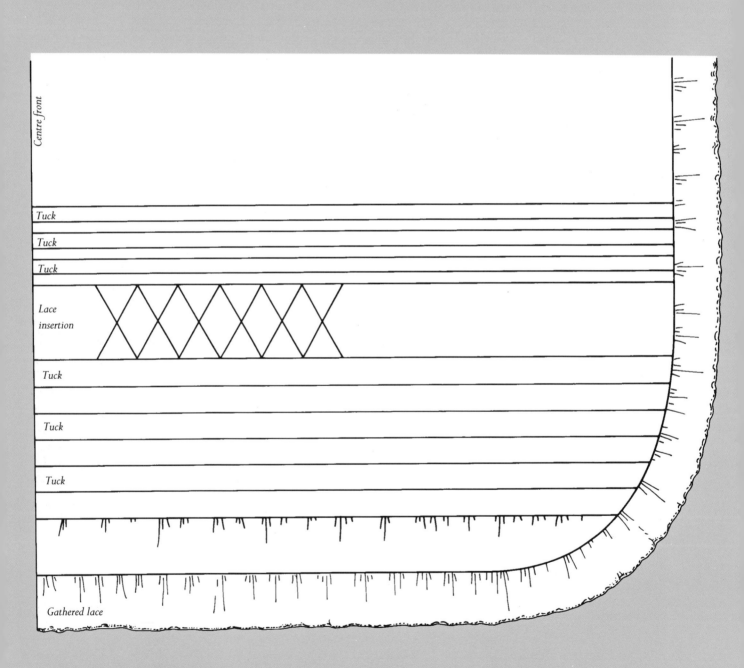

waistband. Pin the other end of the straps to the waistband, 1 centimetres from the edge, enclosing them (and the lace edging) in the insertion lace. The straps should measure 14.5 centimetres.

Cut 1 metre of lace edging and gather it close to the edge. Now whip the lace onto the top of the apron. Start at one end of the waistband, then go around the ouside of the strap, the front neck, the other strap and around the bottom of the waistband, finishing with a mitred corner where you started. Take care not to stitch through the insertion lace at the narrow ends of the waistband, as the ribbon will be threaded through the waistband betwen the lace and muslin. Vary the gathering so it is very tight across the front neck and waistband and very loose around the straps. Use a strong thread and small stitches, since this sewing must hold the gathers of the front neck edge firm.

Skirt tucks On the upper skirt piece (16 x 39 centimetres), press a fold 1.5 centimetres from the edge on the long side for the first tuck and stitch with running stitch or by machine,4 millimetres from the fold. Press a fold 12 millimetres above this stitching line and stitch. Press another fold 12 millimetres above the last stitching, so you have three tucks.

Take 39 centimetres of lace insertion; roll the bottom edge of the skirt under and whip it to the lace insertion.

The tucks on the lower skirt sit on a curved hem, so if you are sewing these by hand I suggest that you tack them first then cut the curve from your corner template and then sew them with a running stitch. If you are machining, then the stitching will probably survive being cut later. On the lower skirt piece, press a fold 17 millimetres from the edge for the first tuck. Stitch 7 millimetres from the fold for the lower skirt tucks. Fold a second tuck 21 millimetres from the stitching line of the first one. Fold a third tuck 21 millimetres from the stitch-

ing line of the last.

Roll the top edge of the lower skirt over and whip it to the bottom edge of the insertion lace, which will join the skirt pieces together.

Gather 48 centimetres of edging lace to measure 35 centimetres and, rolling the lower skirt hem under, whip the lace and fabric together.

Now cut the lower skirt edge the same shape as the template.

Gather 1.35 metres of edging lace to 95 centimetres. Roll the apron skirt edge under and whip the lace to the apron simultaneously.

Turn the top of the skirt over 5 millimetres and run a gathering thread, in a small, neat running stitch, along to pull the skirt (excluding the frill) in to measure 8 centimetres. Now hem the skirt onto the waistband on the wrong side.

Finally thread the ribbon through the insertion lace at the waistband.

Doll, 'Charlotte'
c. 1870 English/Australian
Wax, cotton, human hair
47 x 35.5 centimetres
Historic Houses Trust of New South
Wales, Vaucluse House, Sydney

The handsome wax doll illustrated here was given to a young girl in England about 1850. It still has an extensive wardrobe, which includes two dresses, shawl, apron, flannel petticoat, underbodice, split drawers and bonnet. Some of these garments were probably made for the doll by the owner herself.

Photograph Peter Henning
No pattern

The Tasmanian Lace Exhibition

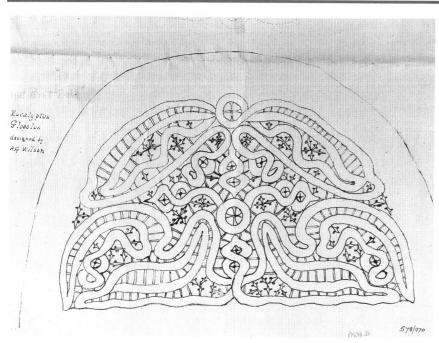

Eucalyptus globulus
Design for tape lace tea cosy
c. 1910 Tasmanian
Designed by Miss A.G. Wilson
Ink on paper
268 x 154 millimetres
Tasmanian Museum and Art Gallery,
Hobart
No pattern

In 1938, the Tasmanian Museum and Art Gallery received a bequest that comprised a collection of lacework and designs from a former Hobart resident, Miss Ada Grey Wilson. The 'few bits of lace and patterns' had been exhibited at the Tasmanian Lace Exhibition, held at the Masonic Hall in Hobart, on 15 September 1910.

Miss Wilson, the daughter of a former premier of Tasmania, Sir James Milne Wilson, had been the hard-working president of a small group, formed in 1908 and committed to the establishment of a school of lace design in Tasmania. The minutes of the committee's first meeting record their intentions:

Lace making has now attained a fair degree of proficiency in Tasmania, and it is thought that the time has come to endow it with a distinctive style of its own. The value of all Arts and Crafts is greatly enhanced when given a national or local character...To further the development of local characteristics and to hasten the time when Tasmania may have well defined laces of her own...it is proposed that a school of lace design be encouraged by holding an exhibition in the summer of 1910.[1]

The committee's plans were a reflection of a worldwide revival in lacemaking, exemplified by its exploitation in women's fashion during the Edwardian era. In Australia, since Federation, the pursuit for the establishment of local and national characteristics in the arts and crafts had been the aim of a number of enthusiastic groups, including the Tasmanian Arts and Crafts Society, which held its first exhibition in Hobart in 1903.[2]

The lace exhibition was envisaged as a catalyst for a lace industry that would feature 'Tasmanian points', employing motifs inspired by the island's flora and fauna. With plans underway, the lacemakers were given their instructions.[3] Open to men and women either born or resident in Tasmania, the competition required that designs be original and incorporate a Tasmanian motif. Each work was to make use of a Tasmanian design, but not necessarily that of the maker. Judging was based on the merits of both design and execution, with a weighting towards good design.

Lace was to be worked in several categories: bobbin, flat point bobbin, needlepoint, needlerun and Carrickmacross. Suggestions for design in each category included Tasmanian wildflowers, birds, insects, animals, figures and scenes. Use of figures and landscapes was, however, discouraged for bobbin lacework, 'owing to the extreme difficulty of execution'. Needlerun lace (which can be identified with Limerick lace), it was agreed, allowed the widest scope for interpretation. Designers were encouraged to use simple motifs for 'small work' and church work, while more complex designs could better be exploited in elaborate pieces such as fans. Continuous patterns were considered appropriate for bobbin lace. Motifs, such as sprays and birds, could be worked first then united with bobbins on the pillow. To achieve richness in the design, lacemakers were asked to employ a variety of stitches such as flat point, Honiton and Maltese. Silk thread, saffron-tinted, or butter-coloured lace, and other outrages of good taste' were excluded. Coloured laces are always more or less barbaric'; it was believed that the right colour for lace was pure unbleached thread.

After two years of preparation, the exhibition opened with fifty local lacemakers contributing a total of fifty-three items of lace work and fifty-six designs. Five hundred lace exhibits were displayed, one hundred and nine of which were inspired by Tasmania's flora and fauna. The majority of works featured native flora, the designs including *Clematis, Snow Berry, Ti-tree, Orchid, Eucalyptus,* and *Waratah.*[4] Miss M. Hope's handkerchief insert, *Purple Creeper and Wild Weed* (right), incorporates the love creeper *(Comesperma volubile),* which is common to the highlands and forest areas of south-eastern Australia. For her tape lace cosy pattern, Miss Wilson chose the gumnut of the Tasmanian bluegum *(Eucalyptus globulus)* and embraces it within the winding tape. Miss Wilson also worked the lace fan illustrated on page 39.

The *Weekly Courier* of 22 September 1910 acknowledged the prizewinners, but lamented that the exhibition remained open for only five and a half hours. Miss Wilson was thanked for her efforts and attributed with having established a lace industry in Tasmania. Such warm comments anticipated a dream that was never fulfilled. Thwarted by the advent of war, which 'stopped all such fancy work', Miss Wilson had also to concede that the prevailing enthusiasm for 'artificial lace which is so easily produced' had rung the death knell on her plans for a school of lace design.

In making her bequest, thirty years later, it was Miss Wilson's hope that local lacemakers might wish to embroider from her designs 'by the yard, in coloured silks' or 'on tablecloths'.[5] The design included in this book will, in some small part, help to sustain her dream.

1. Minutes of Meeting, Tasmanian Lace Ehibition Committee, source, venue and date unknown. Courtesy of the Queen Victoria Museum and Art Gallery.
2. Social Life in Hobart, by Erica, *Weekly Courier,* 19 September 1903.
3. Minutes of Meeting, Tasmanian Lace Ehibition Committee, source, venue and date unknown. Courtesy of the Queen Victoria Museum and Art Gallery.
4. *Tasmanian Lace Exhibition,* 15 September 1910, exhibition catalogue, J. Wach & Sons, Printers, Hobart. Courtesy of the Tasmanian Museum and Art Gallery.
5. Correspondence, Letter to the Curator, Tasmanian Museum and Art Gallery from Miss Ada Grey Wilson, June 1938. Courtesy of the Tasmanian Museum and Art Gallery.

Purple creeper and wild weed
Design for needlerun handkerchief corner
c. 1910 Tasmanian
Designed by Miss M. Hope
Ink on paper (design)
19 x 20 centimetres
Tasmanian Museum and Art Gallery, Hobart

PURPLE CREEPER AND WILD WEED LACE

Mary Laur

*M*iss M. Hope's design for a handkerchief corner was for needlerun lace, as it was called in the Tasmanian exhibition, though the technique is now perhaps better known as Limerick lace. In this lace style, the motifs are worked in thread on net. The original design was for the large handkerchief of the early twentieth century, but here it has been adapted for smaller modern handkerchief.

Finished Size

Handkerchief 27 x 27 centimetres, width of lace edge 5 centimetres

Materials

❖ 36 x 36 centimetre piece of fine cotton net
❖ 21 x 21 centimetre piece of linen or a handkerchief
❖ No. 26 tapestry needle
❖ No. 30 DMC broder machine thread
❖ Embroidery hoop, 25 or 30 centimetres diameter
❖ Artline fine water-erasable pen
❖ Tracing paper
❖ 40 x 40 centimetre piece of calico, with a centre hole cut out smaller than the hoop size

Detail of an adaptation of Purple creeper and wild weed lace c. 1910, 1989.
Original design by Miss M.Hope, adapted by Marie Laurie
Cotton and linen
Width of lace 5 centimetres
Maker's collection

The lacemaker here has adopted Miss Hope's design to make a corner and edge for a modern-sized handkerchief.

Photograph David Liddle

Method

Preparation for working Pre-shrink th net. Trace all the pattern onto the tracin paper.

Place the design and an extra piece c tracing paper under the net, making sure th horizontal grain line of the net lines up wit the edge of the pattern. This is most impor tant! Baste the papers and net together, work ing the basting stitches around the edges of th pattern, but do not sew over pattern area. Fo extra firmness, work a few extra stitche around individual patterns of the design.

Place the calico with the cut window hol over the design part to be worked and put th layers into the embroidery frame. The calicc prevents the hoop stretching the net and split ting the tracing paper.

Working the design Take a long length o thread, double it and then thread both the cu ends through the needle eye. Now there is a loop at the other end. To commence work, pick up a bar of the net on a straight part of the design, and put the needle through the loop. This will anchor the thread and a knot will not be required.

First, outline all the design in running stitch, weaving over and under each bar of the net in turn, that is, work from one hole to another in the net. Once the outlining is completed, fasten off the thread by weaving one thread forward and one back on the pattern line. If possible, always try to stop and start on a straight line. After this first step of the outlining of the design, all the other working steps or processes can be carried out in any order.

For the needlerun fillings, a single thread is used. To start, whip along the edge of the run-ning stitch edge (disguising your stitches if necessary) for approximately 1 centimetre, before commencing the chosen filling. Finish the thread in the same way.

Centre

Corner motif (actual size)

Border motif (actual size)

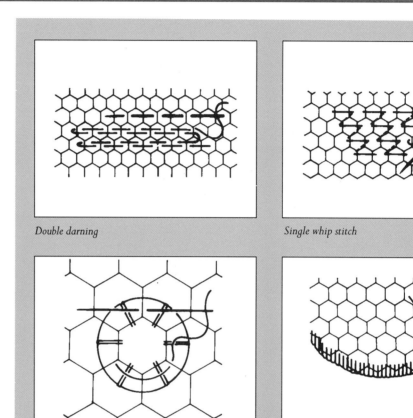

Double darning

Single whip stitch

Working a pop

Work buttonhole stitch edging (enlarged for clarity): work 2 stitches only into each mesh hole.

Any one of numerous needlerun fillings could be used here, but it should be noted that double darning will give the density required for design filling shown in the photograph. Double darning and whip stitch were used in the sample sewn.

Single whip stitch can be worked on a diagonal. Make sure the needle is directly under the bar of the diagonal, as shown in the diagram, working in a step-wise direction.

Pops, or buttonhole rings, are worked by darning around the centre mesh hole and then working two buttonhole stitches into each outside mesh. To finish off pops, whip into two outside loops at the edge of the buttonhole stitches.

The outside edging is worked in buttonhole

stitch, over the outline running stitch (two stitches to each mesh hole).

Remove the completed work from the embroidery hoop before removing all the basting stitches.

Finishing

Attach the worked lace to a piece of linen by tacking the material firmly under the net. Work a running stitch edge as a base, then closely buttonhole stitch over the net and onto the linen.

Press the finished piece on the wrong side, then cut the net closely to the edge on the right hand side. Turn the work over, and trim off the linen (on the wrong side).

Marie Laurie

CARRICKMACROSS COLLAR

Finished size

Inside edge of collar 60 centimetres, width 5 centimetres

Materials

❖ 45 x 55 centimetre piece of fine cotton net
❖ 45 x 55 centimetre piece of cotton organdie or very fine cotton muslin
❖ No. 40 crochet cotton (a coarse thread)
❖ Sylko no. 50 or a single thread of stranded embroidery cotton, or DMC broder machine (reel) no. 30 (fine thread)
❖ No. 10 crewel needle
❖ Tracing paper, white and blue
❖ Outline pen, water-erasable type
❖ Carrickmacross scissors (if available), or sharp-pointed embroidery scissors

Method

Preparation for working Pre-shrink the organdie and net. Trace all the pattern lines onto white tracing paper, using a strong, bold design line, as it must be clear enough to show through both the net and organdie.

Baste the blue tracing paper, paper pattern, net and organdie together (in that order). Work from the centre outwards, making sure the tacking does not pass through any of the pattern with organdie motifs, only spaces.

Working the lace Thread a needle with fine thread and on the inside part of the design commence with a few little running stitches. Over this lay a couching thread, holding it exactly over the design line with your left thumb. Now, oversew the couching thread down with fine thread in small slanting stitches fairly close together through the net and organdie only, not the pattern. The slanting stitches allow the thread to bog down into the thicker thread, making it less obvious. Use a fine thread for couching for flower petals or leaf veins.

To finish a heavy thread and commence a new

Carrickmacross is an appliqué lace, in which fine organdie or muslin is sewn to net. The excess organdie is cut away, leaving the scattered motifs stitched to the surface of the net. The Carrickmacross collar here uses simplified motifs from Alice Cay's fascinator. Alice Cay made her fascinator around 1870, some time before the Tasmanian Lace Exhibition was organised.

thread, overlap both ends for about 1 centimetre and oversew them down firmly. Try to use an outlining thread long enough to avoid joins.

The outside edge of the collar is finished with traditional twirling. With the fine thread commencing as before, hold the coarse thread with your left thumb, and make a clockwise twirl or loop in the thread. With your right hand, oversew the twirl down with two stitches, then two stitches on the edge after this twirl and before the next. Then make another loop or twirl. The loops should be about 5 millimetres in diameter and touching each other. Remember to work two stitches inside the loop and two between.

At the neck edge, buttonhole the net and organdie together in close even stitches.

When the couching and edge are completed, take out the tacking stitches and remove the paper pattern from the back of the work. Press before cutting. Cut away the surplus organdie from the net at the couching lines. This is the most important stage, as one careless snip of the net and will ruin the work.

Now work 'pops' on the net in the places indicated in pattern. These are worked by darning around the centre mesh hole and then working two buttonhole stitches into each outside mesh. To finish off, whip into two outside loops of the buttonhole edge.

Cut away outside edge of organdie and net. Take care not to cut any of the twirls.

Press on the wrong side. If you wish to make this a detachable collar, sew clear plastic press studs at intervals along the neck edge and in the same places on the dress or blouse.

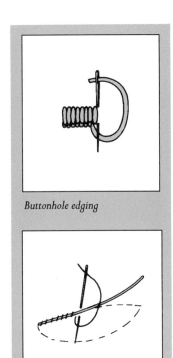

Buttonhole edging

Oversewing the couching thread

61

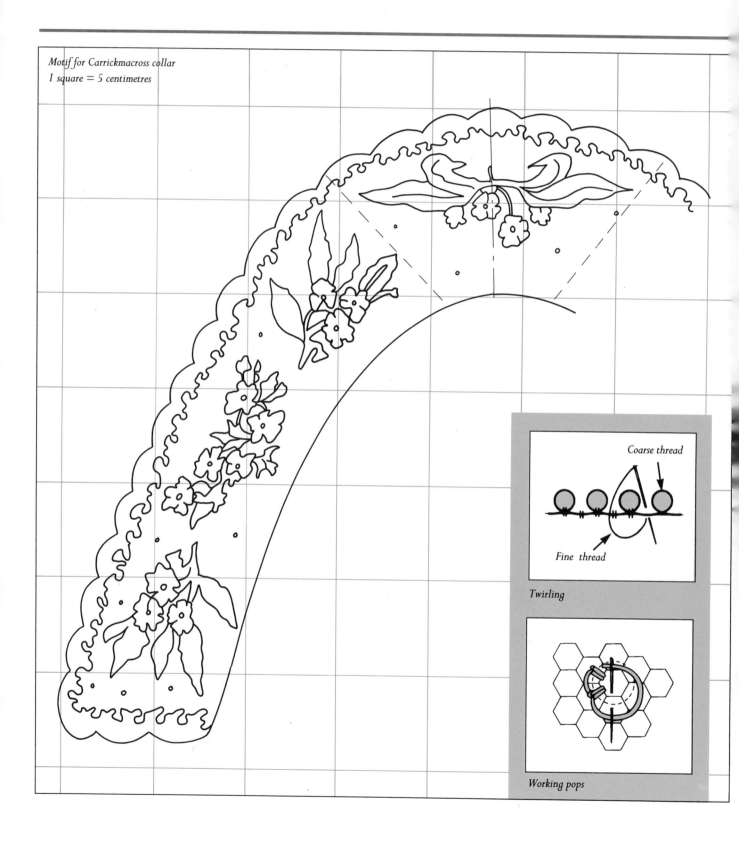

Motif for Carrickmacross collar
1 square = 5 centimetres

Coarse thread

Fine thread

Twirling

Working pops

Crochet

The early history of crochet is difficult to trace, largely because it has been transmitted through the generations by demonstration rather than written instructions. Also, because fabrics are perishable, very few survive, and so textile historians have only fragmentary evidence to study. Different sources suggest a remarkable variety of supposed origins for crochet, including ancient Egypt, the Arabian Peninsula, and South America.

In Europe, the history of crochet is intertwined with that of knitting and lacemaking. Crochet and lacemaking were generally known as nun's work, since nuns have practised and taught these skills for many generations. The word 'crochet' is in fact from the French for hook, and it seems probable that it was French nuns who first used a hook to make crochet and who gave the art its name.

Crochet was brought to Australia from Europe within the cultural baggage of the first women settlers. It was traditionally learned at home, one of the many forms of domestic needlework, both plain and fancy, passed on with love from one generation to another. Unlike embroidery, lace and knitting—which have all been mechanised—crochet has remained a hand method. Therein lies a deal of its charm. Crochet is adaptable, portable and flexible; it is also very quick to do, and lends itself to being worked in units that can later be joined together into a larger whole. In spite of its basic simplicity, crochet offers considerable scope for individual expression. It can be used as a decorative trimming, for example on underwear and babywear, collars, cuffs, handkerchiefs and pillowcases, or to make entire objects, such as a scarf or tea cosy, jug cover, tablecloth or coverlet.

Crochet, like knitting and needlepoint lace, is one of a small group of techniques for producing fabric through the manipulation of a single continuous thread. Because of its chained construction, crochet is very adaptable for decorative open work and is best understood as a member of the lace family—although often dubbed its poor cousin. In Australia, where designers such as Mrs Edwin Field worked hard to improve its prosaic image, crochet has a special place. It was more readily attainable for Australian women than traditional lacemaking, which required extensive training and was very time-consuming. Jennifer Isaacs has commented that 'In Australia, by far the majority of heirloom lace objects are crocheted lace, as this was easily taken up by a woman at home using one metal hook. Patterns imitated the more upmarket forms of needlepoint and bobbin lace.'[1]

In the late eighteenth and early nineteenth centuries in Australia, needlework supplies were hard to come by. Although cotton thread had been available in England since around 1770, it was extremely expensive. During the nineteenth century, however, the price decreased steadily, and by about 1840 plentiful suppplies of inexpensive cotton thread were obtainable in Australia. Because of the accessibility of crochet skills and the ready availability of materials, crochet could be taken up as a creative and productive outlet by women of even minimal means. This resulted in the widespread production of crocheted lace and other items by women from all levels of society.

At the 1879 Sydney International Exhibition, a separate Ladies Court was set up for the display of women's work, including crochet, and in the early years of the twentieth century several exhibitions and competitions of women's arts and crafts were held, frequently in country areas. One of the most important of these was the First Exhibition of Women's Work held in Melbourne in 1907. Following the International Exhibition, and with the rise of nationalism in the late 1800s leading up to Federation, many designers and makers made use of indigenous flora and fauna as design ele-

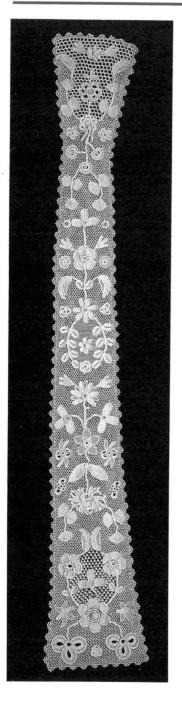

ments in architectural decoration and in the decorative arts. Some particular favourites were flannel flowers, waratahs, wattle and eucalyptus leaves. This trend was not seen in the needle arts, however, until the period from around 1900 to 1914, when locally designed needlework became firmly established in Australia.

The 1979 catalogue from The D'oyley Show: An Exhibition of Women's Domestic Fancywork includes a summary of the development of Australian crochet designs in the early years of this century, and discusses the work of individual crochet designers and makers.[2] Although interrupted briefly by the war years, the emphasis on Australian motifs and design resurfaced in the 1920s, when patterns by Muriel Arnold, Clare Keddy, Bertha Maxwell, Eirene Mort, Gertrude Moore, Grace M. Valentine and others were increasingly available, satisfying a craze for indigenous designs in embroidery and filet crochet. Needlework flourished. Several designers chose to remain anonymous and published patterns under pseudonyms such as 'Playfair', 'Edith' and the fanciful 'Fairy Wax Flower'. 'Playfair', whose designs appeared throughout the 1920s in the *Australian Woman's Mirror*, often used Australian themes for her filet crochet. A 1928 design by her called *Corroboree* is probably derived from Aboriginal motifs.[3]

During the nineteenth and early twentieth centuries, a much higher proportion of people lived in rural and outback Australia than now, and many women led very isolated lives. This placed a weight of importance on mail order services, and on the circulation of women's journals and pattern books. Numerous magazines published locally designed patterns, including *Australian Home Journal* (1894–1928), the *New Idea* (1902–11), *Everylady's Journal* and the *Women's Budget* (1906–37). In addition, both English and American patterns and journals were readily available and widely consulted;

access to these accounts for the high percentage of surviving objects made to English designs from Weldon's Fancywork Series in particular.

The star-patterned doily, for which a pattern is given on page 67, was made during the early twentieth century, and is probably from an Australian pattern. The blue beads around the outer edge identify it as as a jug cover; the beads are not only decorative, but also practical, as they act as weights to keep the doily in place and protect the jug's contents from the inevitable blowflies. Quite a few of these whimsical three-dimensional pieces survive in public and private collections, bearing witness to the numbers that were actually made. Cup and saucer forms like this one were by far the most popular, but teapots and milk jugs also appeared on jug covers. All draw attention to the importance of what Jennifer Isaacs calls 'the Australian Tea Ceremony'.[4]

Filet crochet and Irish crochet were particular favourites in Australia. Filet crochet, which is almost always done with white cotton, is easy to do, is adaptable for works that range widely in scale, and is particularly suitable for creating designs based on a graph. In addition to geometric patterns and figurative images, filet lends itself particularly well to lettering. After the outbreak of war in 1914, women's craft skills were mainly concentrated on nationalistic works and themes, and patriotic slogans proliferated on filet crochet domestic textiles. Many of these carried highly evocative phrases, such as 'Unity is Strength', 'Our Heroes', 'Anzac for Valour', 'Bravo Australia' and 'Bless our Brave Boys'. The teacosy illustrated here is a wonderful example of filet crochet; its design also refers to the tea ceremony and is very typical of those made in the first decades of the twentieth century.

One of the best-known filet designers of that period was Mary Card. She was born in Victoria in 1861, and after studying at the

National Design School for a year, taught English and history, until forced to give up teaching when she became profoundly deaf in her late thirties. In about 1908, when crochet was enjoying a real vogue, she began to design for *Everylady's Journal*. Her patterns for filet crochet, which drew extensively on Australian flora and fauna, were so successful that Mary Card Design Books and Mary Card Giant Charts were also published. In 1912, *The Weekly Times Book of Australian Filet Crochet* came out; it featured designs produced for a competition, and contained about twenty original Australian designs. During the war years, utilitarian work, such as knitted socks and caps for soldiers, took precedence over fancywork, although many filet crochet commemorative pieces were made and Mary Card publications, at least, continued throughout the period.[5]

Whereas filet crochet is typically flat and worked in one piece, Irish crochet is composed of separately crocheted raised motifs, frequently flowers, leaves and birds. These motifs are then joined together in a crocheted mesh ground to form the whole. The combination of firm motifs with the open delicate ground is striking, and characteristic. Irish crochet, or Irish lace, is not Irish by origin, but was probably derived from southern Europe, possibly in imitation of Spanish lace. Cotton and linen thread were usually used, and sometimes silk, while hooks were generally made from bent wire inserted into a piece of wood.

Irish crochet played a vital role in rescuing the ravaged Irish economy after the great famine of the 1840s. In order to help women provide for their families, the sisters of Blackrock Convent in County Cork taught local women to make lace with a crochet hook. The rapid transmission of Irish crochet during the famine was greatly helped by the initiative of a Mrs Roberts from County Kildare, who taught crochet only on condition that her pupils in turn taught thirty

others. Irish crochet was produced by impoverished families throughout the country, many of whom saved the money they earned for a passage out of Ireland, generally to America.

The technique was used to make a wide variety of objects, and although the quality of the work inevitably varied, many exquisite collars, cuffs, bags, parasol covers, dress fronts, bonnets, coats and fichus still survive in museum collections and glory boxes. In Australia, Irish crochet was produced throughout the nineteenth century, and has been widely used by Catholic nuns to create altar frontals and the deep lacy borders for church vestments that are often embellished with religious symbols.

The Irish crochet dress front illustrated here is a fine example from the collection of the Museum of Applied Arts and Sciences and dates to around 1900. It belonged to Nellie Oliphant, who was a dancer for the Australian theatrical company of J.C. Williamson's. Faithful to the high esteem in which lace is so typically held, Miss Oliphant treasured her Irish crochet, wrapping it carefully in tissue paper and storing it away for many years.

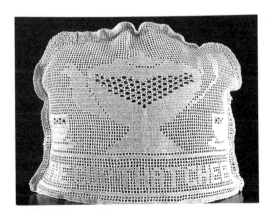

1. Jennifer Isaacs, *The Gentle Arts,* Lansdowne Press, Sydney, 1987, p. 96.
2. *The D'oyley Show: An Exhibition of Women's Domestic Fancywork* catalogue, Women's Domestic Needlework Group, Sydney, 1979, p. 7ff.
3. *The D'oyley Show*, p. 11.
4. *The Gentle Arts*, p. 525.
5. *The D'oyley Show*, p. 8.

DRESS FRONT
c. 1900 Unknown origin
Designer and maker unknown
Cream cotton
134 x 23 centimetres
Museum of Applied Arts and Sciences, Sydney
This beautiful insertion for the front of a woman's princess-line dress was worked in Irish crochet by an unknown maker. The pattern includes leaf motifs and stylised flowers, with delicate three-dimensional stamens joined in a variety of diamond mesh grounds. The as-new condition suggests that this lovely piece may never have been used. According to Nellie Oliphant's great-niece Margaret Marjosan, to whom she gave the piece in the 1950s, it was one of Miss Oliphant's treasures.

Photograph Penelope Clay
No pattern

TEACOSY
c. 1925 Australia
Made by a woman from Mudgee
White cotton
35 x 35 centimetres
Museum of Applied Arts and Sciences, Sydney

This teacosy, is made in filet crochet with a finely scalloped edging. The design features an elegant teapot with pedestal base and curling spout, flanked on either side by a cup and saucer. Across the bottom is the legend 'The cup that cheers'. Women have found an extraordinary variety of ways in which to decorate domestic needlework relating to tea. As well as teacosies, these included table and tray cloths, doilies, throw-overs and aprons.

Photograph Penelope Clay
No pattern

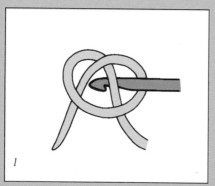

Making a slip loop to start

Completing slip loop

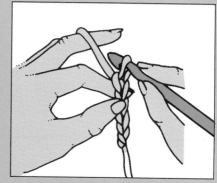

Working a chain

Slip stitch
Insert hook into foundation chain, wind yarn around hook, and draw yarn through chain and loop on hook in one movement

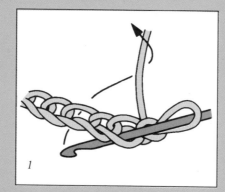

Double crochet
1 Insert hook into foundation chain and follow arrow to twist yarn around hook. Draw loop of yarn through chain so there are two loops on hook.

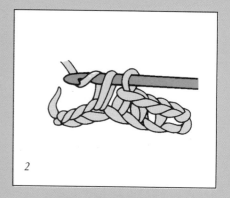

2 Take yarn over hook again and draw it through the two loops on hook.

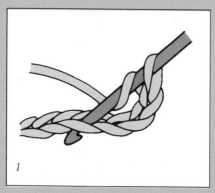

Treble crochet
1 Take yarn over hook, and insert hook through foundation chain.

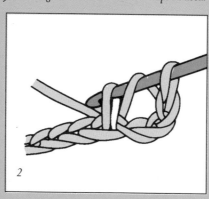

2 Draw yarn through foundation chain to make three loops on hook.

3 Take yarn over hook and draw through only first two loops on hook. Leaves two loops on

4 Take yarn over hook and draw through two remaining loops on hook. Leaves one loop on hook, and you are ready to start next stitch.

Double treble
1 Take yarn twice over hook and insert hook through foundation chain, pull yarn through so there are four loops on needle.

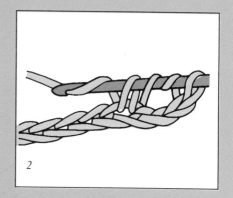

2 Take yarn around hook and pull it through first two loops on hook (three loops on hook). Repeat twice more (two loops, then one loop left on hook).

CUP AND SAUCER MILK JUG COVER

Abbreviations

ch chain

dc double crochet

st stitch

dtr double treble

ss slipstitch

tr treble

sp space

Materials

❖ Mercer crochet cotton, no. 60
❖ Crochet hook, size 1.00 or 0.75
❖ 36 beads

Method

Cup

6 ch join into a ring.

1st row 12 dc into ring.

2nd row 2 dc into every st.

3rd row 1 dc into every st.

4th row 2 dc into every st.

5th to 11th rows 1 dc into every st.

12th row 4 ch (for 1st dtr), 1 dtr into same st *2 ch, 2 dtr into same st, miss 2 sts, 2 dtr into next st, repeat from*.

13th row 2 dc into loop between dtr, 1 dc into each of the next 2 sts.

14th to 16th rows 1 dc into each st. Before ending off, work handle, 18 ch, take back to 6th row of cup with ss. Work 5 dc over ch and into side of cup and then work into ch loop only, 12 dc, 4 tr, 6 dc. Fasten off.

Saucer

1st row Work a row of dc into 3rd row of cup (24 sts).

2nd and 3rd rows 1 dc into every st.

4th row 2 dc into every st.

5th to 8th rows 1 dc into every st.

Novelty crocheted doilies and jug covers like this one were a much-loved part of the ritual of afternoon tea in the 1930s. Out of favour for many years, we can once again appreciate their appeal today. This pattern will make the cover shown in the photograph.

9th row 1 dc into first st, 2 dc into next st. Repeat.

10th and 11th rows 1 dc into every st.

12th row Same as row 12 of cup.

13th row Same as row 13 of cup.

Next 3 rows 1 dc into every st. Fasten off.

Cover

1st row Join thread into 4th row of saucer and work 1 dc into every st (48 sts).

2nd row 1 dc into every st.

3rd row 1 dc into first st, 2 dc into next st, repeat.

JUG COVER
c. 1930 Probably Australian
Designer and maker unknown
Cream cotton with blue plastic beads
Diameter 234 millimetres
Museum of Applied Arts and Sciences,
Sydney

Photograph Penelope Clay
Illustrated in colour on page 40

67

4th to 7th rows 1 dc into every st.

8th row Same as 3rd.

9th to 12th rows 1 dc into every st.

13th row 1 dc into first 2 sts, 2 dc into next st, repeat (144 sts).

14th row 5 ch* miss 1 st, 1 tr, 2 ch, repeat from* and finish off with a ss into 3rd of 5 ch.

15th row 4 ch, 3 dtr into first sp, 4 dtr into next sp* miss 2 sps, 4 dtr into next 2 sps, repeat from * and ss into top of 4 ch.

16th row 7 tr on dtr of previous row, 2 ch, 1 tr between dtr, 2 ch, repeat.

17th row 6 tr, 2 ch, 1 tr, into first sp, 2 ch, 1 tr, into next sp, 2 ch, repeat.

18th row 5 tr, 2 ch, 1 tr into next 3 sps, 2 ch, repeat.

19th row 4 tr, 2 ch, 1 tr into next 4 sps, 2 ch, repeat.

20th row 3 tr, 2 ch, 1 tr into next 5 sps, 2 ch, repeat.

21st row 2 tr, 2 ch, 1 tr, into next 6 sps, 2 ch, repeat.

22nd row 1 tr between 2 tr, 2 ch, 1 tr into next 7 sps, 2 ch, repeat.

23rd row 1 tr, 2 ch into each sp.

24th row 2 dtrgr into first sp, 2 ch, 2 dtrgr into same sp, miss 1 sp, repeat.

25th row 1 tr, 2 ch* 1 tr into V sp, 2 ch, 1 tr between groups of dtr, 2 ch, repeat from*.

26th row ss to centre of sp,* 8 ch, miss 1 sp, 1 dc into next sp, repeat from*.

27th row ss to centre of loop,* 8 ch, 1 dc into next loop, repeat from*.

28th row ss to centre of loop,* 9 ch, 1 dc into next loop, repeat from*.

Break off and thread beads onto ball of cotton.

29th row 4 dc into first loop, 14 ch, slip one bead onto ch, 1 dc into next loop, 14 ch, 1 bead, 4 dc into next loop, 8 dc into next loop, repeat.

This completes the cover.

BUTTERFLY TRIANGLE IN FILET CROCHET

Finished size

Long edge worked in no. 40 cotton measures about 50 centimetres (in no. 20 cotton the triangle would be larger)

Materials

❖ Mercer crochet cotton no. 20 and
❖ Crochet hook size 1.00 *or*
❖ Mercer crochet cotton no. 40 and
❖ Crochet hook size 0.75

Abbreviations

ch, chain; tr, treble; ltr, long treble (double treble); dc, double crochet; h, hole; slst, slipstitch. A 'hole' is 2 ch (following a tr stitch), and 1 tr in the third following stitch of the previous row. The full number of a group of tr stitches is given, and this must be understood to include the tr stitch of the previous 'hole'.

Method

Commence with 230 ch.

1st row 1 tr into 8th ch, 73 more h, then 1 ltr into the end stitch —this is the sloped side — 3 ch, turn.

2nd row 1 tr on 2nd tr, 73 h, 5 ch — this forms the first hole of next row — turn.

3rd row (3 h, 4 tr) twice, (23 h, 4 tr) twice, 16 h, then 1 ltr into the end tr, 3 ch, turn.

4th row 1 tr on 2nd tr, 2 h, 16 tr, 7 h, 10 tr, 9 h, 16 tr, 7 h, 10 tr, 9 h, 16 tr, 7 h, 10 tr, 1 h, 10 tr, 2 h, 5 ch, — for the first hole of next row — turn.

5th row (3 h, 4 tr), twice; 7 h, 22 tr, 9 h, 4 tr, 7 h, 22 tr, 9 h, 4 tr, 7 h, 19 tr, 1 h, 1 ltr in end tr, 3 ch turn.

6th row 1 tr on 2nd tr, 5 h (7 tr, 15 h, 7 tr, 5 h) twice; 7 tr, 8 h, 4 tr, 5 h, 5 ch, turn.

The straight edge is always turned with 5 ch to form the first hole of the next row, so this instruction will be omitted in future rows.

7th row 3 h, 4 tr, 3 h, 4 tr, 5 h (7 tr, 7 h, 7 tr, 13 h) twice; 7 tr, 5 h, 1 ltr as before, 3 ch, turn.

8th row 1 tr on 2nd tr, 5 h (7 tr, 11 h, 7 tr, 9 h) twice; 7 tr, 3 h, 10 tr, 1 h, 10 tr, 2 h.

9th row (3 h, 4tr) twice; 3 h(7 tr, 11 h, 7 tr, 9 h) twice; 7 tr, 5 h, 1 ltr as before, 3 ch, turn.

10th row 1 tr on 2nd tr, 5 h, 7 tr, 7 h, 7 tr, 5 h, 7 tr, 6 h, 7 tr, 7 h, 7 tr, 12 h, 7 tr, 11 h.

11th row 11 h, 7 tr, 13 h, 7 tr, 5 h, 7 tr, 6 h, 13 tr, 5 h, 7 tr, 5 h, 7 tr, 5 h, 1 ltr, 3 ch, turn.

12th row 1 tr on 2nd tr, 5 h, 22 tr, 6 h, 4 tr, 1 h, 7 tr, 1 h, 10 tr, 3 h, 22 tr, 14 h, 16 tr, 8 h.

13th row 7 h, 19 tr, 6 h, 7 tr, 7 h, 16 tr, 3 h, 16 tr, 1 h, 10 tr, 2 h, 4 tr, 4 h, 16 tr, 5 h, 1 ltr, 3 ch, turn.

14th row 1 tr on 2nd tr, 14 h, 7 tr, 1 h, 4 tr, 1 h, 10 tr, 1 h, 10 tr, 13 h, 13 tr, 10 h, 7 tr, 6 h.

15th row 5 h, 7 tr, 11 h, 4 tr, 1 h, 7 tr, 1 h, 10 tr, 10 h, 19 tr, 2 h, 10 tr, 13 h, 1 ltr, 3 ch, turn.

16 th row 1 tr on 2nd tr, 9 h, 10 tr, 1 h, 10 tr, 1 h, 16 tr, 10 h, 16 tr, 1 h, 10 tr, 2 h, 4 tr, 9 h, 7 tr, 4 h.

17th row 3 h, 7 tr, 11 h, 7 tr, 1 h, 4 tr, 1 h, 10 tr, 1 h, 10 tr, 11 h, 7 tr, 1 h, 10 tr, 1 h, 7 tr, 1 h, 7 tr, 7 h, 1 ltr, 3 ch, turn.

18th row 1 tr on 2nd tr, 6 h, 13 tr, 3 h, 7 tr, 15 h, 19 tr, 2 h, 10 tr, 11 h, 7 tr, 3 h.

19th row 3 h, 7 tr, 8 h, 10 tr, 1 h, 10 tr, 1 h, 16 tr, 12 h, 7 tr, 1 h, 4 tr, 2 h, 10 tr, 1 h, 7 tr, 6 h, 1 ltr, 3 ch, turn.

20th row 1 tr on 2nd tr, 7 h, 16 tr (5 h, 4 tr) twice; 7 h, 7 tr, 1 h, 10 tr, 1 h, 7 tr, 1 h, 7 tr, 7 h, 7 tr, 3 h.

Filet crochet consists of blocks of trebles separated by spaces of individual trebles and chain stitches. The most important point to remember in filet crochet is to keep an even tension at all times. The butterfly triangle featured here appeared in a Needlecraft Practical Journal (price threepence) published in England during the First World War. The triangle was intended for a corner of a tablecloth (or for all four courners).

21st row 3 h, 7 tr, 7 h, 13 tr, 3 h, 7 tr, 9 h, 10 tr, 8 h, 4 tr, 1 h, 19 tr, 5 h, 1 ltr, 3 ch, turn.

22nd row 1 tr on 2nd tr, 4 h, 7 tr, 1 h, 7 tr, 2 h, 4 tr, 9 h, 4 tr, 6 h, 7 tr, 1 h, 4 tr, 2 h, 10 tr, 1 h, 7 tr, 7 h, 7 tr, 4 h.

23rd row 5 h, 7 tr, 8 h, 16 tr, 5 h, 4 tr, 14 h, 4 tr, 3 h, 16 tr, 3 h, 1 ltr, 3 ch, turn.

24th row 1 tr on 2nd tr, 3 h, 10 tr, 23 h, 4 tr, 1 h, 19 tr, 6 h, 7 tr, 6 h.

25th row 7 h, 7 tr, 5 h, 7 tr, 1 h, 7 tr, 2 h, 4 tr, 24 h, 4 tr, 3 h, 1 ltr, 3 ch, turn.

26th row 1 tr on 2nd tr, 26 h, 4 tr, 3 h, 16 tr, 4 h, 7 tr, 8 h.

27th row 9 h, 7 tr, 4 h, 10 tr, 30 h, 1 ltr, 3 ch, turn.

28th row 1 tr on 2nd tr, 14 h, 4 tr, 3 h, 4 tr, 11 h, 4 tr, 4 h, 7 tr, 10 h.

29th row 11 h, 7 tr, 14 h, 10 tr, 1 h, 10 tr, 12 h, 1 ltr, 3 ch, turn.

30th row 1 tr on 2nd tr, 12 h, 4 tr, 3 h, 4 tr, 15 h, 7 tr, 11 h.

31st row 3 h, 4 tr, 7 h, 7 tr, 7 h, 4 tr, 9 h, 4 tr, 13 h, 1 ltr, 3 ch, turn.

32nd row 1 tr on 2nd tr, 10 h, 4 tr, 3 h, 4 tr, 6 h, 10 tr, 6 h, 7 tr, 6 h, 10 tr, 2 h.

33rd row 3 h, 4 tr, 7 h, 7 tr, 7 h, 4 tr, 6 h, 10 tr, 1 h, 10 tr, 8 h, 1 ltr, 3 ch, turn.

34th row 1 tr on 2nd tr, 8 h, 4 tr, 3 h, 4 tr, 16 h, 7 tr, 10 h.

35th row 9 h, 7 tr, 29 h, 1ltr, 3 ch, turn.

36th row 1 tr on 2nd tr, 25 h, 4 tr, 3 h, 7 tr, 8 h.

37th row 7 h, 7 tr, 3 h, 10 tr, 23 h, 1 ltr, 3 ch, turn.

38th row 1 tr on 2nd tr, 17 h, 4 tr, 3 h, 16 tr, 3 h, 7 tr, 6 h.

39th row 5 h, 7 tr, 4 h, 7 tr, 1 h, 7 tr, 2 h, 4 tr, 17 h, 1 ltr, 3 ch, turn.

40th row 1 tr on 2 tr, 16 h, 4 tr, 1 h, 19 tr, 5 h, 7 tr, 4 h.

41st row 3 h, 7 tr, 7 h, 16 tr, 5 h, 4 tr, 11 h, 1 ltr, 3 ch, turn.

42nd row 1 tr on 2nd tr, 11 h, 7 tr, 1 h, 4 tr, 2 h, 10 tr, 1 h, 7 tr, 5 h, 7 tr, 3 h.

43rd row 3 h, 7 tr, 4 h, 13 tr, 3 h, 7 tr, 14 h, 1ltr, 3 ch, turn.

44th row 1 tr on 2nd tr, 10 h, 7 tr, 1 h, 10 tr, 1 h, 7 tr, 1 h, 7 tr, 4 h, 7 tr, 3 h.

45th row 3 h, 7 tr, 5 h, 10 tr, 1 h, 10 tr, 1 h, 16 tr, 7 h, 1 ltr, 3 ch, turn.

46th row 1 tr on 2nd tr, 5 h, 19 tr, 2 h, 10 tr, 7 h, 7 tr, 4 h.

47th row 5 h, 7 tr, 6 h, 7 tr, 1 h, 4 tr, 1 h, 10 tr, 1 h, 10 tr, 3 h, 1ltr, 3 ch, turn.

48th row 1 tr on 2nd tr, 3 h, 16 tr, 1 h, 10 tr, 2 h, 4 tr, 4 h, 7 tr, 6 h.

49th row 7 h, 7 tr, 6 h, 4 tr, 1 h, 7 tr, 1 h, 10 tr, 3 h, 1 ltr, 3 ch, turn.

50th row 1 tr on 2nd tr, 6 h, 13, tr, 5 h, 7 tr, 8 h.

51st row 9 h, 7 tr, 5 h, 7 tr, 6 h, 1 ltr, 3 ch, turn.

52nd row 1 tr on 2nd tr, 11 h, 7 tr, 10 h.

53rd row 11 h, 7 tr, 9 h, 1 ltr, 3 ch, turn.

54th row 1 tr on 2nd tr, 8 h, 7 tr, 11 h.

55th row 3 h, 4 tr, 7 h, 7 tr, 7 h, 1 ltr, 3 ch, turn.

56th row 1 tr on 2nd tr, 6 h, 7 tr, 6 h, 10 tr, 2 h.

57th row 3 h, 4 tr, 7 h, 7 tr, 5 h, 1 ltr, 3 ch, turn.

58th row 1 tr on 2nd tr, 5 h, 7 tr, 10 h.

59th row 9 h, 7 tr, 5 h, 1 ltr, 3 ch, turn.

60th row 1 tr on 2nd tr, 5 h, 7 tr, 8 h.

61st row 7 h, 7 tr, 5 h, 1 ltr, 3 ch, turn.

62nd row 1 tr on 2nd tr, 5 h, 7 tr, 6 h.

63rd row 5 h, 7 tr, 5 h, 1 ltr, 3 ch, turn.

64th row 1 tr on 2nd tr, 5 h, 7 tr, 4 h.

65th row 3 h, 7 tr, 5 h, 1 ltr, 3 ch, turn.

66th row 1 tr on 2nd tr, 4 h, 7 tr, 3 h.

67th row 3 h, 7 tr, 3 h, 1 ltr, 3 ch, turn.

68th row 1 tr on 2nd tr, 2 h, 7 tr, 3 h.

69th row 3 h, 7 tr, 1 h, 1 ltr, 3 ch, turn.

Now finish with holes to a point, then work 4 dc in each chain loop on sloped side.

General Instructions

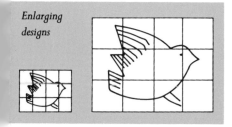

Enlarging designs

Enlarging patterns

Wherever possible, we have provided full-size patterns to be traced and transferred to your fabric. When this has not been possible, diagrams have been supplied on a grid for enlarging. To enlarge the pattern, you will need to draw up the final size of the design and divide it into a grid. If the grid in the book is described as 1 square = 2 centimetres, then draw up a 2 centimetre grid. Once the grid is prepared, copy the design section by section onto it, making each part correspond to the original. The pattern can, in fact, be enlarged to any size you want: if you draw up a 4 centimetre grid, for instance, you will produce a pattern twice the suggested size.

Patterns may also be enlarged by photocopying. This method can be used for embroidery and appliqué patterns, though care should be taken, as enlarging in this way may distort the pattern. *Never enlarge templates for piecing in patchwork, as great precision is needed here. Even a very small amount of distortion will prevent pieces going together properly.* If you want a larger block, redraft the pattern instead.

Mitred corners on hems

Press the fold lines of the hems, turning the hems to the wrong side. Open out the fabric again and fold the corner over diagonally, to the point where the two folds meet, to form a 45 degree angle. Press lightly. Trim corner to above 5 millimetres from the fold (1). Turn under the raw edges of the hems, and turn up the hems. Sew the mitre invisibly or with small overcast stitches, then stitch the hems in the usual manner.

Methods of transferring designs

Tacking method Use this method on textured fabrics. Trace the design onto tissue paper using a sharp, hard pencil. Pin the tracing onto the fabric with the right side facing up. Use machine sewing thread to work running stitches through the paper and the fabric. When tacking complete, use the point of your needle to score through the paper along the stitching line, taking care not to damage the fabric. Carefully remove the paper.

Dressmaker's carbon paper Use this method on smooth-textured fabrics. It is

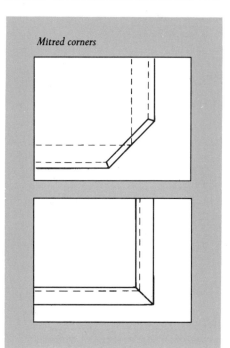

Mitred corners

ideal for complex designs. Place the fabric on a firm surface. Position the design on top of the fabric and secure in place. Slide the dressmaker's carbon paper, shiny side against the fabric, under the design. Use a tracing wheel or a worn-out ballpoint pen to draw over the lines. Lift a corner of the design to check that the design is being transferred.

Water-soluble-ink pens These can be used on washable, light-coloured fabric. Place the original design under the fabric, and trace the design onto the fabric. It is very important to wash away the ink completely with *cold* water. Heat will set the ink permanently, so do not press your work before removing the ink.

Pencil tracing A pencil can be used to lightly trace designs onto light-coloured fabric, with the design placed under the fabric. Use an F pencil.

Using an embroidery hoop

Embroidery hoops come in a variety of sizes. Choose one that is large enough that you don't need to keep moving it, but not so large that it is awkward to use. Bind the inner ring of the hoop with cotton tape. This helps to protect your fabric and also prevents the fabric from slipping in the hoop. Place the inside ring into place. It is important to ensure that the fabric is held taut, with the grain lines straight.

Using a rectangular frame

You may use a slate frame or a simple picture frame or artist's stretcher. A slate frame has two rollers which have webbing attached. These slot into two straight arms and are secured with wing nuts. The fabric can only be as wide as the webbing. Neaten the sides of the fabric by folding back 1.5

cm and stitching them close to the fold. Centre the top and bottom sides of the fabric against the webbing and attach by oversewing. The sides may then be laced to the side bars of the frame for added tension. If using a picture frame or artist's stretcher, the fabric is simply stapled to the frame.

Blocking embroidery

Embroidery that has been slightly distorted during working may benefit from blocking. This procedure will not always compensate for poor workmanship, so always stitch with care to avoid excessive distortion of the fabric. Use a piece of caneite and cover it with a sheet of clean white paper. Dampen the fabric by misting it with water. Use rustproof drawing pins to pin your fabric out onto the board, putting the pins into the excess

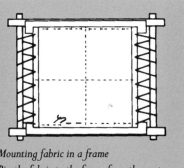

Mounting fabric in a frame
Pin the fabric to the frame from the centre out in both directions. Stitch from the centre out keeping the grain of the fabric straight. Then lace the sides with a nylon, wool or linen thread.

fabric at the edges of the embroidery. Do not pin within the area of the article itself. Stretch the fabric tight and make sure that the grain lines are straight and at rightangles to one another. Leave the embroidery on the board until it is completely dry.

Stretching and blocking canvaswork

Stretching the work After the work is completed it should be stretched. With cold water dampen the canvas and pull it in the opposite direction from the way it has been drawn up during stitching. If the piece has not been worked in a frame, quite a lot of stretching may be needed.

Blocking After stretching and while the canvas is still damp, use a set square to check that the horizontal lines of the stitching are perpendicular to the vertical lines. Place a piece of brown paper on a board, fastening it down with masking tape on the edges. Draw up the original shape of the canvas, for example, a cushion cover 36 x 36 centimetres, on the brown paper, marking the centres of each side. Pin the work to the board with drawing pins. Working

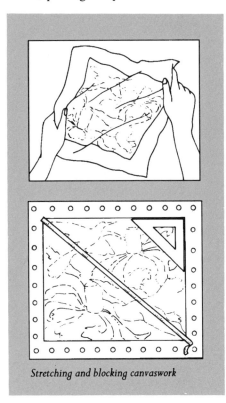

Stretching and blocking canvaswork

from the centre of one side, pull the canvas firmly to the centre of the opposite side and pin. Extend the pinning outwards to the corners. Allow the canvas to dry at room temperature before removing it from the board.

Mounting finished work

When the embroidery is complete remove the work from the embroidery frame. At this stage you will need a piece of boxboard or masonite to mount the embroidery on. Stretch the embroidery across the board ready to lace the edges on the back. Use masking tape to hold the work as a temporary measure while lacing the embroidery. It is important when lacing to use a strong thread that does not break easily. Start in the centre of the frame with your needle threaded on the ball of wool or thread. Do not cut it into short lengths when you have reached the edge. Start at the centre again and stitch to the other edge. Tighten both sides of the lacing, keeping an even surface on the front of the work. Turn the work around and lace across the other side.

To give a good finish to the work, neatly slipstitch a piece of calico or matching fabric in place covering the back of the work.

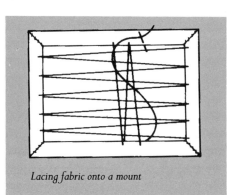

Lacing fabric onto a mount